What the Gospels Meant

ALSO BY GARRY WILLS

What Jesus Meant

What Paul Meant

Saint Augustine (A Penguin Lives biography)

Saint Augustine's Confessions (translation)

The Rosary

GARRY WILLS

What the
Gospels Meant

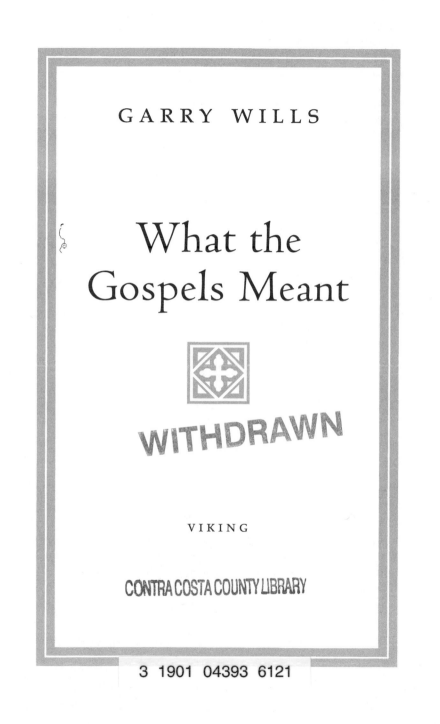

VIKING

VIKING

Published by the Penguin Group

Penguin Group (USA) Inc., 375 Hudson Street, New York, New York 10014, U.S.A. • Penguin Group
(Canada), 90 Eglinton Avenue East, Suite 700, Toronto, Ontario, Canada M4P 2Y3 (a division of Pear-
son Penguin Canada Inc.) • Penguin Books Ltd, 80 Strand, London WC2R 0RL, England Penguin
Ireland, 25 St. Stephen's Green, Dublin 2, Ireland (a division of Penguin Books Ltd) • Penguin Books
Australia Ltd, 250 Camberwell Road, Camberwell, Victoria 3124, Australia (a division of Pearson
Australia Group Pty Ltd) • Penguin Books India Pvt Ltd, 11 Community Centre, Panchsheel Park,
New Delhi – 110 017, India • Penguin Group (NZ), 67 Apollo Drive, Rosedale, North Shore 0632,
New Zealand (a division of Pearson New Zealand Ltd) • Penguin Books (South Africa) (Pty) Ltd, 24
Sturdee Avenue, Rosebank, Johannesburg 2196, South Africa

Penguin Books Ltd, Registered Offices: 80 Strand, London WC2R 0RL, England

First published in 2008 by Viking Penguin, a member of Penguin Group (USA) Inc.

10 9 8 7 6 5 4 3 2 1

Grateful acknowledgment is made for permission to reprint selections from *The New English Bible*.
Copyright © Oxford University Press and Cambridge University Press, 1961, 1970. Used by permission of Cambridge University Press.

LIBRARY OF CONGRESS CATALOGING-IN-PUBLICATION DATA

Wills, Garry,———.
    What the Gospels meant / Garry Wills.
        p. cm.
    ISBN 978-0-670-01871-0
    1. Bible. N.T. Gospels—Criticism, interpretation, etc. I. Title.
    BS2555.52.W55 2007
    226'.06—dc22   2007023128

Printed in the United States of America

Set in Aldus • Adapted from a design by Francesca Belanger

TO RAYMOND BROWN

devout scholar

Contents

Key to Brief Citations

The four Gospels are cited as Mt, Mk, Lk, and Jn.

1B Raymond E. Brown, S.S., *The Birth of the Messiah: A Commentary on the Infancy Narratives in Matthew and Luke*, new updated edition (Doubleday, 1993)

2B Raymond E. Brown, S.S., *The Gospel According to John*, 2 volumes, continuously paginated (Doubleday, 1966, 1970)

3B Raymond E. Brown, S.S., *An Introduction to the Gospel of John*, edited by Francis J. Maloney (Doubleday, 2003)

4B Raymond E. Brown, S.S., *The Death of the Messiah*, 2 volumes, continuously paginated (Doubleday, 1994)

M Joel Marcus, *Mark 1–8* (Doubleday, 2000)

New Testament translations are by the author. Jewish Scripture is quoted from *The New English Bible* (Oxford University Press, 1970)

Introduction: What Is a Gospel?

IN A BOOK, *What Jesus Meant*, I drew indiscriminately from all four Gospels to find the true Jesus. Some objected that the different Gospels are formed from different traditions, or different layers of tradition, some more authentic than others, some truer or closer to historical reality. I argued then, and will again, that the church was right to consider all of the Gospels as authentic, with the only kind of authenticity they sought or recognized.

They are not historically true as that term would be understood today. They are not history at all, as our history is practiced. They do not draw on firsthand testimony or documents. They do not use archives—for instance, court records for the trial of Jesus, birth records for his genealogy, or chronological markers for his time line. They were composed four to seven decades after the Resurrection. They culminate an oral preaching process. They use the methods and symbols and theology of the writings their authors held to be history par excellence—the Sacred History of the Jews, recorded in their Sacred Writings (*Graphai*, "Scripture").

To understand this, we must go back to the earliest part of

what would later be known as the New Testament, Paul's seven genuine letters. "The New Testament" did not exist when Paul wrote—any more than it would exist, decades later, when the evangelists wrote. He and they had only one Bible, and they preached from it. Paul would have been horrified had he been told that his occasional letters would be lumped in with other matters as a new Bible, one that could be distinguished from the one he knew and revered. He is the first to record the proto-creed of the followers of Jesus: "As my first concern, I passed on to you what had been passed on to me, that Messiah died for our sins, *in accord with the Sacred Writings;* and that he was buried; and that he arose on the third day *in accord with the Sacred Writings*" (1 Corinthians 15.3–4, emphasis added). This is the basic Announcement (Kerygma) that would be the test of orthodoxy. It is the nucleus from which the Gospels were built up.

Paul, and his predecessors in the thirties of the first century CE, preached from the Jewish Sacred Writings that Jesus is the Jewish Messiah. The Gentiles, too, were saved by the Jewish Messiah, since all rescue comes from the Jews (Romans 11.26). The Gentile believers in the risen Jesus are the seed of Abraham, the fulfillment of the prophecy that he would be the father of many nations (Romans 4.17—"Gentiles" means "Nations"). We are given a glimpse into the earliest liturgies of the Brothers and Sisters in Luke's tale of disciples going to Emmaus, disappointed that Jesus had been killed after "we trusted that he would be the one to set Israel free" (Lk 24.21). The stranger who has joined them asks:

"Are you so little prompt of mind or eager of heart to grasp what all the prophets voiced, how the Messiah had to suffer and to enter into his splendor?" And *starting from Moses* [*the Law*] *and all the prophets,* he expounded for them the passages *in all the Sacred Writings* that led to him. (24.25–27, emphasis added)

This description of the preaching in the first gatherings is followed by the liturgical sequel, the Eucharist. First, the stranger (who is Jesus) makes as if to "pass on beyond" the disciples (24.28)—which is a sign of divine unapproachability in the Sacred Writings. When Moses asked the Lord to show him his glory, God responded:

"My face you cannot see, for no mortal man may see me and live." The Lord said, "Here is a place beside me. Take your stand on the rock and when my glory passes by, I will put you on a crevice of the rock and cover you with my hand until I have passed by. Then I will take away my hand, and you shall see my back, but my face shall not be seen." (Exodus 33.20–23)

That was in the era of Moses, of the Promise. But in the era of Jesus, of the Promise fulfilled, the Messiah reveals himself: The disciples urge the stranger to linger with them, since night is coming on (the time for celebrating the Passover, and the Lord's Meal). Staying with them, he breaks bread and offers it to them, "when their eyes were opened and they recognized him" (24.31). After they eat the bread of union, they rejoice: "Was our heart not on fire in us as he spoke to us along the road and *opened out the Sacred Writings?*" (24.32).

There we have an artistic rendition of what the early gatherings of believers did in their meditations on the meaning of Jesus. It shows us how the preaching, praying, communing, and rejoicing disciples met to reflect how Jesus had fulfilled Jewish hopes. It was in such gatherings that the Gospels were gestated. There the oral memories of what Jesus had said and done were turned over and over in the light of the Sacred Writings. Out of such sessions were the memories of Jesus sifted and ordered, not simply in terms of what memories were available to any gathering but how those memories were understood. There were two principles of selectivity—looking forward to the Passion and Resurrection, and looking backward to the Jewish history, destiny, and legacy. The concern was with both where Jesus was going (to death and glory) and where he came from (the whole Jewish development of the Promise).

Building backwards from the Passion, one Gospel, Mark's, reached back to begin from the baptism of Jesus, where the last prophet, John the Baptist, plays the role of Elijah as precursor to the Messiah (Mk 9.11–13). This link with the line of Sacred History is carried back even farther in the two Gospels that tell of Jesus' birth: Matthew has the child re-enact the Exodus from Egypt, and Luke has the child fulfill priestly hopes in the Temple. John's Gospel travels even farther back, beyond the birth of Jesus, where the Word is seen as God's Wisdom, according to the Sacred Writings. Everything writ-

ten is an attempt to "situate" Jesus in the entirety of Sacred
History.

What, then, is a Gospel? The genre has often been debated.
The Gospels are not biographies, or history books, or treatises.
Their shape is determined by their uses, by their place in the
lives and memories and prayers of the early believers. They
are themselves a form of prayer. It was once said that Jesus
began as biography and ended as creed. We now know that
the reverse of this is true. He begins in the life of the church
as Paul encountered and reported it—in the Eucharistic formula, the Kerygma, the baptismal hymn, and the hymn to
Jesus' divinity, which are first given us in 1 Corinthians 11.23–
26, 15.3–4, Galatians 3.26–28, Philippians 2.5–11. These are
the earliest records of what was known and believed about
Jesus shortly after his Resurrection. They begin with a "high
Christology," a belief in Jesus' divinity. Biographical memories are fitted to them only later, when the Gospels get written. Those biographical memories were present from the
outset, but were put in order only as they conformed to the
most important fact about Jesus—that his Resurrection proved
that he was the Messiah. To understand this, constant recourse
had to be made to the Sacred Writings.

Proof of this as the organizing principle of Christian
preaching and liturgy is seen in the earliest examples of Christian art. Some critics have expressed surprise that the catacomb and mausoleum art of the early centuries is at first
almost entirely taken from the Jewish Sacred Writings, not
from what we now call the New Testament. Abraham, Moses,
Noah, Jonah, the three men in the fire, Daniel, the patriarch

Joseph, Job—these were the popular figures.[1] "Initially these Old Testament figures flooded Christian art, to the point even of taking over and dominating it for an extended period."[2] The early believers do not picture the Resurrection of Jesus. They knew he had risen. They and their friends had seen the risen Jesus (more than five hundred of them according to our earliest report, 1 Corinthians 15.6). But what did that fact *mean*? It fulfilled the "sign" of Jonah risen after three days from the whale (Mt 12.39–41). In the same way, the meaning of baptism was conveyed by Moses striking water from a rock.[3] The Sacred Writings are not taken as "proof texts" to establish biographical facts about Jesus. Believers know and believe the facts about Jesus' life. But the meaning of that life is impossible to read outside the context of the Sacred Writings.

The importance of this fact is established by the formation of the canon of authoritative Gospels. That was a defensive move. The canon was not set up to compete with or replace the Sacred Writings. The Gospels are commentaries on and continuations of the Sacred Writings. It is unfortunate that they have been separated by later usage. We should avoid when we can the terms "Old Testament" and "New Testament." Then why was the canon set up in the first place? It was to distinguish trustworthy books from the Gnostic writings *which denigrated the Jewish Sacred Writings*—they treated the Yahweh of Genesis as Yaldaboath, who created the vile world.[4] The canon was formed not to replace the Jewish Sacred Writings but to defend them from those who were attacking them.[5] The Gnostic Gospels also denied or denigrated parts of the Kerygma—the real death of Jesus, the need for him to be resurrected (e.g., Gospel of Philip 68). They opposed fleshly reality in the name of a higher spirituality. That was a part of their opposition to the "lower" superstitions of the Jews. There is a vogue for the Gnostics now, but they were an elite and snobbish company. The four canonical Gospels create a far more complex and challenging vision. It is a testimony to the common sense of the early church, as well as to the providential guidance of the Spirit, that the four Gospels were defended against those who would have dismissed them—this is the real sense of "inspiration" when that term is applied to the canonical works.

What is a Gospel? It is a meditation on the meaning of Jesus in the light of Sacred History as recorded in the Sacred Writings. The meditation is a communal act, incorporating the preaching and prayers of many Christians, partly born out of and partly intended for the early liturgies. It is an application of the continuing Sacred History to the particular situations of the Gospel writers. The books reflect not only past events from the life of Jesus but his experienced life in the members of his community. This concept of the community as the mystical body of Christ was not a late development. It was a settled point of agreement to which Paul could appeal in the forties and fifties of the first century: "As we have in our body many members, and all the members do not perform the same function, so we, though many, are one body in Messiah, and serve as members of each other. . . . You are Messiah's body, each a member with a function." (1 Corinthians 12.12–14, 18). This belief was asserted in the earliest baptismal hymn that Paul quotes:

Baptized into Messiah,

you are clothed in Messiah,

so that there is no more

Jew or Greek,

slave or free,

man and woman,

but all are one, are the same

in Jesus Messiah. (Galatians 3.26–28)

Given this sense of Jesus' indwelling in the community, its members did not ask what Jesus would be saying if he were present. It asked what he *is* saying because he *is* present. As each Gospel was a continuation of the Sacred Writings, so it was a continuation of the life of Jesus being lived in his members. If the community was suffering persecution or doubt or trouble, it took strength in the fact that this was the suffering of Jesus, who had known fear at Gethsemane and Golgotha, who had known divisions in his following, who had been betrayed. The Gospels thus find Jesus present in persecution (Mark), in instruction (Matthew), in consolation (Luke), and in mystical exaltation (John). These different emphases are not the only things found in the relevant Gospels, but it may be helpful to look first at them as an entry into the various ways the life of Jesus was experienced in his members. So I will begin by seeing Mark as the book of the suffering body of Jesus, Matthew as the book of the teaching body of Jesus, Luke as the book of the reconciling body of Jesus, and John as the book of the mystical body of Jesus. We rejoin each of the four gatherings as we read them. We find how they center themselves on their principle of life, the ever-present Jesus. Though the Gospels as a whole are an authentic presentation of this living Savior, we gain particular insights from each gathering as we join it to read its book.

My aim here is not to go exhaustively into each episode of every Gospel, but to suggest the goal, method, and style of each evangelist. They write in marketplace *(koine)* Greek, and in my translations I stay close to the telegraphic character of that language, even to its clumsy connectives, inconsistent tenses, and other infelicities. Each Gospel writer manages to make of this blunt medium something muscular and awkwardly eloquent, and I try to follow each one's individual approach. There is something profoundly misleading in the prettified "Bible English" of most translations, which offer the serene picture of an ideal life, or a set of oracles from on high, or a doctrinal compendium. These are reports from the Christian life as it was being lived, with all its anguish, hopes, and pleadings. They reach out for assurance from the Sacred Writings, holding Jesus to his promises, probing for what he really meant and was. As such, each is a sophisticated symbolic construct, made of communal experience, joint questioning of the Jewish Scripture, communal self-criticism, and exhortation. Even the most simple of the Gospels, that of Mark, is a complex document of Christian suffering and hope, the voice of a persecuted church staying true to its divine leader, its members reaching out toward Jesus and toward the Jesus in one another. Joining that body in its struggle is not so much "an act of piety" as a testing adventure. We have to enter into a gathering very different from a modern church, into an oral culture resonant with echoes from the omnipresent prophets and psalms, into a world more interested in what a tradition means than in what a document says, a world where Jesus was partly hidden but by no means absent. In order to get back into that world, it may be necessary at first to stress how strange the Gospels must seem to the modern reader, how distant from our literary preconceptions. We journey outward to arrive inward, going through the merely strange to the deeply mysterious. The Jesus of Mystery is at first hidden in the Gospel before being revealed there.

NOTES

1. Andre Grabar, *Christian Iconography: A Study of Its Origins* (Princeton University Press, 1968), pp. 8–10. Walter Lowrie, *Art in the Early Church*, rev. ed. (Harper & Row, 1947), pp. 40, 64–67. When Jesus did start appearing in catacomb art, it was often as the Good Shepherd (Lowrie, pp. 42–43)—an image also derived from the Jewish Sacred Writings (2 Samuel 5.2, Psalm 78.70–71, Jeremiah 23.4, Zechariah 13.7, among many places).

2. Pierre du Bourguet, S. J., "The First Biblical Scenes Depicted in Christian Art," in Paul M. Blowers (editor), *The Bible in Greek Christian Antiquity* (University of Notre Dame Press, 1997), p. 300.

3. Angela Donati, *Pietro e Paolo: La storia, il culto, la memoria nei primi secoli* (Electa, 2000), p. 47. See also 2B 322: "When Moses struck the rock and water flowed from it . . . [that] was the most frequently painted Old Testament symbol in the catacombs."

4. Kurt Rudolph, *Gnosis: The Nature & History of Gnosticism*, translated by Robert McLachlan Wilson (HarperSanFrancisco, 1987), pp. 73–78.

5. The defense of the Sacred Writings by Irenaeus was continued through Ambrose and Augustine into the whole later tradition.

I. MARK

Report from the Suffering Body of Jesus

MARK'S IS THE *shortest Gospel, and it was for centuries the most neglected of the four.*[1] *It is one of the three Gospels that resemble one another—those called Synoptic because they have "a common view" (Greek* synopsis*). Of the three, Matthew was placed first in the traditional order. Since Matthew has more material than Mark, and the material is better organized than either Mark or Luke managed, Matthew was for a long time considered the foundational Synoptic Gospel. Augustine called Mark simply "the drudge and condenser"* (pedisequus et breviator) *of Matthew.*[2] *The humble station of Mark as a kind of biblical Cinderella was stressed by her shabby garb—Mark's Greek is clumsier and more awkward than that used by the other evangelists.*[3] *No wonder his was the least cited Gospel in the early Christian period.*[4] *As if to add insult to injury, one of the most quoted parts of the Gospel was a later addition to it (the so-called Markan Appendix—twelve verses added to its ending).*

That the greatest impact Mark's Gospel has made on church tradition is derived from verses which no modern textual

11

critic would acknowledge as belonging to Mark is no small matter. Among Luther's allusions to Mark in his collected works, almost one fourth are to passages from the spurious ending (16.9–20). The single verse from Mark that has achieved fame because of its place in Luther's Small Catechism—"Whoever believes and is baptized shall be saved" (16.16)—is from the spurious ending.[5]

But this Cinderella got her glass slipper in the nineteenth century, when it was finally noticed that the other Synoptics, Matthew and Luke, cite and use (and correct) Mark, but he does not do the same for them. This obviously meant that he preceded them—his is the first Gospel, setting the pattern for the others. Since that discovery, his has become the most studied and influential Gospel. It is also the Synoptic Gospel that most shows the signs of a particular community as its source and audience—a persecuted community with internal divisions and conflict. This brings it together with the only other New Testament documents written before the destruction of the Temple in 70 CE, Paul's letters to five troubled gatherings.[6]

This may help us understand why the first Gospel was written at all. Paul's normal dealings with the hundreds of gatherings he must have known in his thousands of miles of travel were oral, the expected form of communication in an oral culture.[7] Writing was a difficult and rare act—so difficult that "writers" dictated to scribes, who did the laborious inditing on papyrus rolls. That is why Paul "wrote" to only five communities, under two conditions—that he had to be away *from the community, and that the community needed his intervention in its internal conflicts. In a somewhat similar way, Mark set down the oral teachings that were important to his own community as part of a concerted effort to remind and strengthen and console them in their discord under persecution. The repetition of his message in the liturgies and debates of his fellows was a way of keeping Jesus present through the storm.*

NOTES

1. The number of words in the Greek text of each Gospel is, in rising order:

Mark	11,229
John	15,420
Matthew	18,278
Luke	19,404

Robert Morgenthaler, *Statistik des neutestamentlichen Wortschatzes* (Gotthelf Verlag, 1958), p. 166. Mark's Gospel was originally even shorter than the form in which we have it. The last twelve verses were added to the later manuscripts in two increments, and added in a style foreign to the main body of the work.

2. Augustine, *The Consistency of the Gospel Writers* 1.4.

3. The awkwardness of Mark's language is rather naggingly stressed by John C. Meagher, *Clumsy Construction in Mark's Gospel*, Toronto Studies in Theology, vol. 3 (Edwin Mellen Press, 1979), and in Frans Neirynck, *Duality in Mark: Contributions to the Study of the Markan Redaction* (Leven University Press, 1972). But a measured acknowledgment of the problem is in M 199, 202, 263, 334, 523, 595.

4. In an index to citations from the patristic era, Mark gets only 26 pages of mentions—compared with 37 pages for John, 59 for Luke, and 69 for Matthew. Bruce M. Metzger, *The Canon of the New Testament: Its Origin, Development, and Significance* (Oxford University Press, 1987), p. 262.

5. Donald H. Juel, *Master of Surprise: Mark Interpreted* (Fortress Press, 1994), p. 14.

6. Paul is now credited with seven authentic letters, but one of those is to an individual about an individual (Philemon), and two are to the same community, Corinth.

7. Plato presents the view of an oral culture when he has Socrates contrast "dead" written words with the live interchanges that "write in the soul" (*Phaedrus* 275–76).

1. Persecution in Syria

MARK'S GOSPEL was written in, with, and for a particular
community. It has references that would be meaningless outside a local context—references not picked up by either Matthew or Luke when they are using material from Mark. Some
of these references are quite specific. For instance, when Mark
tells how Simon of Cyrene carried the cross of Jesus, he adds
the information that Simon was "the father of Alexander and
Rufus" (15.21). Obviously these men were familiar to his
community, probably as members or former members of it.
In the same way, during the arrest of Jesus in the Garden of
Olives, "A young man who followed him was wearing nothing over his naked body but a linen cloth, and they tried to
overpower him, but he slipped out of the linen cloth and ran
away naked" (14.51–52). Various scholars have tried, unsuc-
cessfully, to find some symbolic meaning in this mysterious
reference, but it clearly mentions a particular person known
to Mark's hearers. Even Mark's name, later added as the Gospel author, may have had a special local appeal.[1] Other references are less specific, but these too were removed by Matthew
and Luke as having less meaning for the communities they

were addressing. Examples of this are Mark's unique concern with the brothers and sisters of Jesus and with discord in his family, and his mention of women disciples acting from fear.

The local references that most thoroughly pervade the Gospel are pointed mentions of persecution. These passages have special resonance for the people Mark is addressing. There is an intense, almost an obsessive, focus on the community's suffering. Jesus describes in the grimmest terms what his disciples must face:

> "Keep yourselves alert. They will turn you over to the councils, and you will be whipped in the synagogues, and you will be put before governors and kings because of me, to testify before them. And before that time you must announce the revelation to all the peoples. And whenever they arrest you, turning you over, do not worry about what you will say, but whatever is given you at the moment, speak that. For it will not be you speaking but the Spirit, the Holy One. And brother shall hand brother over to death, and father shall hand over child, and children shall stand up against parents and bring them to death, and you will be hated by all because of my claim. But whoever bears up to the end will be rescued." (13.9–13)

What Jesus predicted is actually occurring in the Markan community. Mark gives that away in these words of Jesus: "For those days will press men hard, as never since the beginning of this creation that God created until now, and as may never be" (13.19). This is often taken to be a prediction of the final "tribulation," of the End Time. But the clumsily inserted "until now" *(heos nyn)* and the enigmatic "as may never be [again?]" indicate that Mark is applying the words of Jesus to the situation he and his fellows are sharing as he writes (M 29).

The Lord's Sufferings

WHAT JESUS predicts for his followers must first happen to him:

> "The Son of Man will be handed over to the high priests and the scribes, and they will condemn him to death and hand him over to the [Roman] Gentiles, and they will make sport of him and spit on him and whip him and execute him, and three days later he will rise again." (10.33–34)

Jesus says that brother will betray brother among his followers. His own family has first turned against him. "His relatives went forward to overpower him, for they said, 'He is a madman'" (3.21). People in his hometown say there must be something fake or sinister about him:

> "Is he not merely the carpenter, Mary's son, and the brother of Jacob and Joseph and Judas and Simon? And are not his sisters here in our company?" And he dumbfounded them. And Jesus told them that no prophet lacks honor except in his hometown, *and among his relatives and in his own household.* And he could not do works of power other than by

17

putting his hands on a few who were ill, to heal them. And he was astounded by their lack of trust. (6.3–6, emphasis added)

Jesus supplies a model for those who must renounce their family if it stands in the way of the Revelation:

And his mother and his brothers come, and standing outdoors they sent inside, calling for him. And a crowd was sitting around him, and they tell him, "See! your mother and your brothers outdoors are seeking you." And answering them he says, "Who is my mother, who my brothers?" And looking about at those seated in a circle around him, he says, "Look! My mother and my brothers. Whoever performs what God wills, such a person is my brother and my sister and my mother." (3.31–35)

Mark so connects the idea of family division with persecution (the situation in his community) that he uses persecution in an ironic answer when Peter asks what reward he will get for following Jesus:

Jesus said, "In truth I tell you, there is no one who gives up his home, or his brothers or his sisters, or his mother or his father, or his children, or his lands for my sake, or for the sake of the Revelation, without receiving a hundred times the homes and brothers and sisters and mothers and children and lands—along with persecution—in this present age; but in the age to come, eternal life." (10.29–30, emphasis added)

Jesus connects his own sufferings and those of his follow-ers. "Whoever wants to follow after me must abandon him-self and take up his own cross, and accompany me" (8.34). "Can you drink the cup I drink?" (10.38). Jesus' calm bearing under trial and torture and execution is a model for his fol-lowers as they face their own ordeals—as opposed to the desertion of Peter and others. He speaks of the need of people to be rooted in the Revelation, lest "they be hobbled when hard pressure and persecution come because of the Word" (4.17).

A Divided Community

MARK SPEAKS not only of persecution from without but of defection and betrayal from within. Brother is betraying brother—as happened even with the Lord. Mark alone of the evangelists talks of Jesus' sisters and brothers, and he gives the names of all four brothers. Unlike Jesus himself, they were all named for patriarchs—Jacob and Joseph and Judas and Simon.[2] The most important of these is the eldest, Jacob, who presided over the gathering in Jerusalem during the middle years of the first century (Acts 21.18). "Jacob" is usually translated "James" in English versions of the New Testament, and the same applies to the apostle James the son of Zebedee. Yet English translations of Jewish Scripture retain the form "Jacob."[3] We should use that Hebrew name for the brother of Jesus, to stay aware that Jacob tried to keep the Jerusalem community observant of Jewish Law, which was the cause of his conflict with Paul (Galatians 2.12–14). That kind of conflict must have left its traces in the Markan community, as a source of internal division within the community. The disciples' failures described in the Gospel speak to problems in the gathering that Mark addresses. As Joel Marcus says:

> Mark is the harshest of all the Gospels in its depiction of Jesus' relation to his family, and it is interesting to speculate why. To some extent Mark's portrait of strained relations must be historical; it is probably not the sort of depiction that the church would have created out of thin air, since it seems to put both Jesus and his family in a dubious light. John 7.3, moreover, supports its central point by saying that Jesus' brothers did not believe in him. But Mark's added harshness still needs to be explained, and one popular theory has pointed to evidence that Jesus' family was influential in the pre-70 Jerusalem church, that Jesus' brother James [sic] was strongly identified with a strictly Torah-observant party, and that Peter is associated with this Law-observant party in Gal 2.11–14. Jesus' family, then, and perhaps even the disciples, might represent the Torah-observant Jewish Christian church in Jerusalem against which Mark, as an exponent of Torah-free Gentile Christianity, was battling. (M 279–80)

Raymond Brown reads Mark in the same way:

> One suspects strongly that Mark's addressees must include Christians who have suffered and failed—a community to whom this Gospel offers hope since it points out that Jesus himself did not want to drink the cup and that even his most

intimate disciples failed. Since evangelistic theology is geared to spiritual response, this is a Passion Narrative that will have special meaning for those who have sought to follow Christ but find insupportable the cross that they are asked to bear in life, i. e., to those who at some time have been reduced to asking from the bottom of their hearts, "My God, my God, for what reason have you forsaken me?" (4B 28)

Marcus noted that Peter was associated with Jacob in the conflict with Paul at Antioch (M 279). That may explain why Peter is treated as critically as Jesus' relatives in the Gospel. "Mark's picture of Peter is generally a rather negative one" (M 24). In Mark, Jesus even calls Peter "Satan" (8.33). Peter is blustery in the way he tries to correct Jesus (14.31) and in his boast that all the others may betray Jesus but certainly he will never do so (14.29). We know where that kind of cockiness is leading: "And he [Peter] launched himself, under pain of a curse, into swearing, 'I have no knowledge of the man you mention'" (14.71).

Mark lacks some of the more favorable treatments of Peter in Matthew—for instance, the statement that Jesus will build up his gathering on the "Stone" called Peter (Mt 16.18). Since Mark has no post-Resurrection appearances, he also lacks John's command that Peter should "feed my sheep" (Jn 21.15–17). All this works against the claim, supposedly based on Papias, that Mark was the interpreter of Peter.[4] We know that Christian factions claimed to be of Peter's party (1 Corinthians 1.12). There must have been some dissidents in Mark's community claiming the same thing, which makes Mark point out the weaknesses in Peter, as he had stressed the opposition from Jesus' family.

Where Was the Persecution?

If MARK was written in and for a community under persecution, does he supply any hints about where this was occurring? The older view was that the Gospel was written in Rome, but that was based on the view that Peter had dictated the Gospel to Mark, and Peter died in the Neronian persecution in Rome (64 CE). If that view were a sound one, the Gospel would hardly show such a lack of sympathy with Peter. Besides, the persecution that killed Peter and Paul on the charge of burning Rome down was a brief spasm, not a continuing persecution of the sort the Markan community undergoes.

What does the Gospel itself say about the plight of its auditors? A passage to begin with is this:

> Whenever you see the defilement that desolates, established where he should not be—understand this, reader!—then let those in Judaea run away into the hills. If a man is on his roof, let him not come down and go inside for what he might carry away, and if one has gone into his field, let him not look back to get his coat. But dire the plight of women who are pregnant or nursing in those times. But pray the times come not in winter. . . . Had the Lord not aborted the times, no human flesh had been rescued. But for the chosen of his choosing, he aborted the times. (13.14–18, 20)

Mark alerts those in his audience that he is talking about them ("understand this, reader!"), and also gives them hope that the time of their ordeal has been aborted (literally, "cut back").

What is the defilement that desolates *(to bdelygma tēs erēmōseōs)*? It has often been taken as referring to the destruction of the Temple by the Romans in 70 CE. But elsewhere Mark does not seem to know the circumstances of that destruction, and he does not refer to it directly—as Luke does at 21.20–21: "Whenever you see Jerusalem encircled by armies, then recognize that its desolation impends, then let those in Judaea flee into the hills." Luke, unlike Mark, is clearly writing after the final siege of Jerusalem. Others have taken Mark to be referring to Caligula's threat to erect a statue of himself in the Temple (Josephus, *Antiquities* 18.8), but that threat, issued in 40 CE, was never realized, and it did not prompt a mass flight to the hills.

Luke takes "the defilement that desolates" from Daniel 11.31, 12.11, which describes the pollution of the Temple by Antiochus Epiphanes, who in 168 BCE placed a pagan altar above the altar of sacrifice, which "put a stop to sacrifice and offering" (Daniel 9.27). This is not a parallel to the Romans' total destruction of the Temple, but it does have a parallel in the Zealots' seizure of the Temple in 67 CE, which escalated the Jewish War. The Zealots maintained their military camp in the Temple until it was destroyed. Josephus, the Jewish historian, calls these Zealots "outlaws," *lēstai (Jewish War* 4.138)—the term Jesus uses (Mk 11.17) for those who abuse their roles in the Temple. Joel Marcus argues convincingly that this action of the Zealots in 67 CE and the following years is what prompted the Markan community to "run away into the hills" in Syria, escaping the war that would soon destroy the Temple. The Zealots are the Jews who have been persecuting the Markan community, just as the next wave of Zealots would do, under Bar Kokhba, in 132 CE.

The nearest hills for the persecuted Christians in Judaea to run toward were in the Syrian Decapolis, a Gentile area where Paul had been active. Mark shows Jesus visiting Syria twice, crossing the Sea of Galilee to reach it. If that is indeed where Mark's listeners had run from their persecutors, both of the times when Jesus entered that territory would be rich with personal meaning for them, and Mark's emphasis on the two trips would become more understandable.

Jesus' First Trip to Syria

THE FIRST TRIP into Gentile territory follows immediately on Jesus' use of a parable that describes the gathering-in of the Gentiles. It is the parable of the mustard seed, small at first, that grows into a huge bush where "winged birds of the air find shelter" (4.32). This image of birds for gathering nations is familiar in the Sacred Writings. At Ezekiel 17.23, the Lord takes a tiny slip from a cedar tree which, planted, grows so large that

Winged birds *of every kind* will roost under it,
    they will roost in the shelter of its sweeping boughs.

Ezekiel 31.5–6 describes the Assyrian empire, before pride led to its downfall, as a great cedar of Lebanon:

> Its boughs were many, its branches spread far;
>> for water was abundant in the channels.
> In its boughs *all the birds of the air* had their nests.

Daniel 4.21 describes Nebuchadnezzar, before he was cursed, as a great tree "in whose branches the birds lodged." The parable of Jesus thus says that his reign will gather in the nations. These passages from the Sacred Writings are the kind Mark's community would be meditating on as they recalled the parable of the mustard seed, and its connection with the Gentiles of Syria.

They would reflect on other passages having to do with fear and persecution when they heard how Jesus crossed to Syria over the Sea of Galilee. When a great storm tosses the boat, yet Jesus sleeps peacefully in the tumult, the disciples are panic-stricken. "They woke him up and said to him, 'Teacher! Have you no concern that we are perishing?'" (4.38). This cry would be familiar to the Markan community, since Levites were required to recite Psalm 44.23–24 every day (which is why they were called Wakers):

> Bestir thyself, Lord; why dost thou sleep?
>> Awake, do not reject us forever.
> Why dost thou hide thy face.
>> heedless of our misery and our sufferings?

"And Jesus, awakened, rebuked the wind and told the sea, 'Silence!' [to the wind] and, 'Be bridled!' [to the sea]." Reining in the sea is a divine act, what God does at Genesis 1.9, where he reins the sea back to make land appear. At Job 26.10–11,

> He has fixed the horizon on the surface of the waters,
>> at the farthest limit of light and darkness.
> The pillars of heaven quake
>> and are aghast at his *rebuke*.

At Psalm 104.9,

> Thou didst fix a boundary which they [the waters] might
>> not pass;
> they shall not return to cover the earth.

God speaks at Isaiah 50.2:

> By my *rebuke* I dried up the sea,

Psalm 106.9 says:

> He *rebuked* the Red Sea and it dried up,
>> he led his people through the deeps.

Those last two citations are especially important, since—as we shall see—Exodus imagery runs all through this Gospel. Joel Marcus points out that storms are often an image of persecution, or of war, or of temptation. (Augustine, when he prayed for release from temptation, asked God to quell a frothy sea at its shoreline; *Confessions* 2.3.) The disciples expressing fear at sea are like Mark's community terrified under persecution, and the rebuke at their lack of trust is like that of Moses when he breaks the tablets because of the Israelites' loss of faith while he was on the mountaintop.

Jesus in the boat does not only rebuke the wind and the waves, but chides the disciples, using the harsh word "cowards" *(deiloi).* "Cowards! Are you still without trust?" The disciples are constantly criticized by Jesus for their lack of trust (the kind of trust he showed by sleeping without fear in the storm). When, on another occasion, they fear a crowd will starve in the desert for lack of provisions (as if Jesus could not provide), he says, "Have you a heart of stone? Can your eyes not see? Can your ears not hear? Have you no memory?"

Jesus gives his followers many tongue-lashings, but this one instills a special fear, since the same rebuke he gives them had tamed the storm winds. "They feared with a great fear, and said, one to the other, 'What kind of person is this, if even the wind and the sea do his will?'" This fear is even greater than what they felt during the storm. They are confronted with the scary prospect that God himself is their fellow traveler toward Syria.

On his arrival in Syria, Jesus is greeted by the rush of a demoniac upon him, one who spotted him coming "from far off" (5.6). This man, in an "unclean" land of Gentiles, suffers every kind of ritual pollution. He dwells among tombs, he is uncontrollable, he has burst all chains put upon him, and he challenges Jesus the minute he puts foot on Gentile territory: "What is to me and to you, Jesus, Son of the Most High God?" The devils fence with Jesus in this impure new territory, as the devil had tried him in the desert. When Jesus threatens to cast the devils out of this man, they try to trick him into letting them stay in the region they have made their home. Jesus out-tricks them, casting the devils into pigs on the land—but the pigs rush off the land into the sea.

The fact that this is foreign land is emphasized by the name the devils in the man give themselves. They call themselves "Legion," the title of a Roman military unit of thousands. Moreover, the wild boar was the emblem of the Roman soldiers stationed in Palestine (M 351). Jesus has advanced into a part of the Roman empire outside the realm of the Temple, and what he tells the man he freed is strikingly different from what he tells others he has healed. Normally, he tells any cured person not to relate what has happened (see, later, the "Messianic secret"). But this man, who wants to return with him to Judaea, he orders to stay in the Gentile area: "Turn back to your home, *to your people,* and report to them how great are the things the Lord has done for you, what mercy he has had on you" (5.19). He calls himself the Lord and makes a beachhead for the Revelation in this territory. Nonetheless, the inhabitants ask him to leave. They do not want to be caught in this cosmic struggle. They cannot believe that Jesus acts on his own—he must have power from the devil. He cannot be the Messiah—which is the view that Mark's community will be coping with in Syria.

Jesus' Second Trip to Syria

JESUS' SECOND TRIP to their region is even more weighted with meaning for Mark's people. Jesus has gone over the border of Galilee into the area of Tyre. Marcus points out that there was hostility between Galilee and Tyre, because Tyre consumed much of the agricultural produce of Galilee, where many went hungry. That is the social setting for Jesus' saying to the Gentile woman here who seeks healing for her daughter: "Let the children first be fed, since it is not right to take food from the children and throw it to little dogs" (7.27). The children of the family are Jews and the little dogs are Gentiles. But the mother rises to this taunt with a winning plea: "Lord, even little dogs under the table feed on the children's leftovers" (7.28). Jesus tells her: "Because of what you said, return to your daughter—the demon has gone out of her" (7.29). This is an authoritative sanctioning of Paul's teaching, that salvation is for Jews first, and only then for Gentiles.

Jesus now proceeds "from the Tyrian region, through Sidon toward the Sea of Galilee through the middle of the Decapolis region [of Syria]"—through the territory of Mark's people. Here he meets the deaf-mute and heals him by putting his spittle on his tongue and thrusting his fingers into his ears (7.33–35). This is the obverse of Jesus' charge against the disciples, that they have ears to hear but hear not. This time he does tell the cured man not to speak of his healing—but the man does it anyway, and the word spreads through this Gentile region, where people say, "He has done all things well, and he makes the deaf to hear and the mute to speak" (7.37). The Revelation is resisted in Syria, but it is also spread there. Mark's people are the inheritors of the revealing acts Jesus worked in their area.

NOTES

1. The ascription of Gospels to particular authors did not happen until the second century. Three were attributed to names with special authority—two apostles (Matthew and John) and a supposed companion of Paul. Though some say that the evangelist Mark is the "John Mark" of Acts 12.12, Joel Marcus argues that this figure was so minor that deriving an important tradition from him seems unlikely (M1 18). He guesses that there may have been some memory of a Mark as leading the community addressed in the Gospel, which led to the attribution.

2. Christians have tried to deny that Jesus had brothers and sisters, because they take "born of a Virgin" as a biological, not a theological, datum. But see on the virgin birth chapter 4 below.

3. The odd philological shifts of Greek *Iakobos* and Latin *Iacobus* into Spanish *Iago* and *San Diego*, into English *Jacob* and *James*, introduce too much of later Christian history to be helpful in translating the New Testament.

4. Old-fashioned exegetes tried to salvage the Papias claim—that Mark was Peter's interpreter—by saying that Peter transmitted unfavorable information about himself out of humility. At a time when some Christians—even Paul—were critical of Peter, he would hardly have wanted to supply them with more ammunition.

2. Messianic Signs

BECAUSE OF Mark's crude Greek and his simple linking of clause to clause (parataxis), it was held at one time that he was an artless, even naïve, collector of pre-existing elements, with little to add on his own. That was when all the Gospels were assumed to be pre-Pauline, innocent of theological nuance, more biographical than doctrinal. Paul and John were supposed to have added a "high Christology" (attributing divinity to Jesus) to the story of the simple itinerant preacher from Galilee, one whose acts were recorded by the Synoptics.

But now we know that Paul's letters were written before the Gospels, and that a high Christology existed in Christian circles even before Paul wrote those letters. He quotes baptismal formulas, creedal statements, and hymns that make high claims indeed—like this hymn, from the letter to the Philippians (2.6–11):

> He, having the divine nature from the outset,
>> held it no usurpation to be God's equal,
> but emptied himself out into the nature of a slave,
>> becoming like to man

and in man's shape he lowered himself,
   so submissive as to die, by death on a cross.

For this God has exalted him,
   favored his name over all names,
so at the name of Jesus all knees shall bend,
   above the earth, upon the earth, and below the earth,
and every tongue shall acknowledge
   that Jesus is the Lord Messiah, to the glory of God the
   Father.

That hymn's two equal parts, each of three verses, reflect the double creedal report of Paul as what he received from tradition (1 Corinthians 15.3–4):

That Messiah died for our sins,
   in accord with the Sacred Writings;
   and that he was buried;
and that he arose on the third day,
   in accord with the Sacred Writings

It is not surprising, then, that Mark arranges his entire Gospel to emphasize that Jesus is in fact the Messiah and has divine powers. We have already seen Jesus putting bounds on the sea, like God in Genesis. The Gospel opens with a Messianic scene, of John the Baptist as the herald of the Messiah (1.2–11). John himself says, "A stronger one is coming after me, the thong of whose sandal I am not able to untie" (1.7). As soon as Jesus is baptized, he is identified as Messiah: "And just as he was coming up from the water he saw the heavens being torn up and the Spirit coming down on him as it were a dove" (1.10). The dove coming over the water recalls the Spirit hovering above the waters at the creation (Genesis 1.2). Jesus as Messiah is inaugurating a new order of creation. The tearing up of the heavens is an eschatological sign, as at Isaiah 64.1: "Why didst thou not rend the heavens and come down?" When the divine voice from heaven says, "You are my son, my loved one, in whom I delight," this echoes Psalm 2.7, "You are my son," and Isaiah 42.1, "my chosen one, in whom I delight."

Unlike Matthew, Mark does not normally make his references to the Jewish Scripture explicit—he assumes that his hearers know what he is referring to. This is natural, since Paul, the emissary of the Gentiles, preached that Jesus was the fulfillment of the whole Jewish history, of the Law and the prophets. The Brothers (as Christians were known in Mark's time) began their life in the synagogues, and continued there until, gradually, from place to place, they were expelled. Jesus had taught in the synagogue, and Paul kept up that practice. There was not a separate religion called Christianity in this period. The Brothers were Jews who accepted Jesus as the Messiah. When Gentiles were brought to accept this Messiah, he was preached to them as the fulfillment of Jewish expectations and prophecies. Again, Paul proves that. There was not—as some commentators assume—a different Jesus preached to Jews and to Gentiles. The Brothers, in meditating on the life of Jesus, saw it in the context of Jewish destiny. There was only one Bible in their eyes. When separate verses from the Sacred Writings are cited, they are not simple "proof texts," for apologetic purposes. They are part of the whole matrix of the faith in Jesus as the Messiah.

We see this in the very next episode of Mark's Gospel, after the baptism: "And straightway the Spirit casts him out into the desert," where "he was with the wild animals" (1.12–13). Satan comes to tempt Jesus, as he came to the first man and woman, testing them as they lived in the primitive world with the first animals. But where the original human beings failed their test, Jesus prevails, and the whole course of fallen mankind begins its great reversal.

The Messianic meaning of Jesus comes out in every aspect of Mark's story. Here, for instance, is the choice of the Twelve:

> And he goes up into the mountain, and he calls forward those he picked himself, and they broke away to him. And he made their number twelve, for them to be near him, so he could make them emissaries for preaching and for having the authority to cast out demons. And he made their number twelve. . . . (3.13–16)

The words "he goes up into the mountain" are used repeatedly for Moses' ascents of Mount Sinai. At Exodus 24, Moses calls leaders to come up the mountain after him, and then he sets up twelve sacred pillars as symbols of the twelve tribes. For Jesus to appoint the Twelve was to make an eschatological forecast of the recovery of the ten lost tribes—they were to be united to the other two in the End Time. That is when the full Revelation will be preached and all the devils cast out—which is the task to which Jesus dedicates his Twelve.

The New Exodus

THE FOLLOWERS OF Jesus constantly pondered their own religious Jewishness, whether they were born to the faith or came to it as Gentiles. A regular theme of these meditations was to celebrate their own liberating Exodus. As Moses had freed the Israelites from Pharaoh and led them through the wilderness, despite temptations and defections along the way, so Jesus was leading them to the new reign of heaven. This is evident in the way Jesus feeds the five thousand in a new wilderness, re-enacting the miracle of the miraculous bread called Manna. Jesus has withdrawn into a desert space, and the crowd follows him (6.31–34). "He was deeply moved by the crowd, as so many sheep who lacked a shepherd" (6.34). This recalls Moses' prayer at Numbers 27.17 "that the community of the Lord may not be like sheep without a shepherd." "The hour was advanced" (as in the Passover service), and the disciples feared that the crowd, brought out into such a deserted space, would starve.

When Jesus tells the disciples to collect what food there is, they can find only five loaves of bread and two fish. The five loaves recall the five books of Moses, the Pentateuch, since the word of the Law was supposed to be nutritive. The two fish may refer to the two tablets of the Law. Jesus tells the vast throng to "recline for separate food servings on the green grass, and they settled, group by group, in fifty groups of a hundred each" (6.39–40). This recalls how Moses, during the Exodus, separated the people into "units of a thousand, of a hundred, of fifty, or of ten" (Exodus 18.21)—these are units within each of the twelve tribes (Deuteronomy 1.15). As Jesus chose twelve close followers, so the excess food left over after the feeding fills twelve baskets (6.43). This kind of excess, like the hundred gallons of water Jesus turns to wine at Cana (Jn 2.6), is a sign of eschatological fullness. That is the point of all the references to excessive delight in God's final kingdom, the New Jerusalem.[1] When Jesus prays, blesses and breaks the loaves, and distributes the food to thousands by way of his disciples, the scene looks forward to the Eucharist as well as back to Exodus.

Jesus goes directly from this Exodus scene up onto a mountain to pray, while his disciples start out across the Sea of Galilee. A storm comes up so severe that in the early morning hours the disciples are "tortured" at the oars, trying to keep control of their boat, and they lose confidence—as the Israelites lost trust in their God and turned to the Golden Calf while Moses was on the mountain. Jesus knows of their ordeal.

> And toward the fourth watch of the night, he comes toward them, treading along on the water, and he went on to pass them by. But they, when they saw him treading along on the water, concluded he was a ghost and they shrieked, for all of them saw him and were dumbfounded. But straightway he addressed them, and he said. "Take heart. I AM." (6.48–50)

We saw, in the story of the walk toward Emmaus, how "passing by" the disciples is a sign of God's presence. Joel Marcus cites other scriptural passages, based on this model, to show that "the verb *parelthein* ('to pass, to pass by') became almost a technical term for a divine epiphany" (M 426). Given the Exodus pattern in this whole sequence of Mark's Gospel, we should give full force to Jesus' words "Take heart. I AM." This is the divine title used in Exodus 3.13–14:

> Then Moses said to God, "If I go to the Israelites and tell them that the God of their forefathers has sent me to them, and they ask me his name, what shall I say?" God answered, "I AM; that is who I am. Tell them that I AM has sent you to them."

There can be no "higher Christology" than this. Indeed, because of this passage we should probably give the full weight of that "I AM" to Jesus' response when he is investigated by the chief priests. When witnesses against Jesus give inconclusive evidence, the high priest reduces the whole procedure to a single challenge:

> At this point, the high priest asked Jesus, "You! Are you the Messiah, the Son of the Blessed One?" But Jesus said, "I AM, and you will see the Son of Man seated at the right hand of the Power, and arriving with the clouds of heaven." But the high priest, ripping apart his mantle, says at this, "What need is there of witnesses? You have heard this blasphemy!" (14.61–64)

One can say that the high priest had reason for this reaction. He is closer to the truth than are those who speak of "gentle Jesus meek and mild," a simple ethical teacher. As Chesterton put it in *The Everlasting Man:*

> There is more of the wisdom that is one with surprise in any simple person, full of the sensitiveness of simplicity, who should expect the grass to wither and the birds to drop dead out of the air when a strolling carpenter's apprentice said calmly and almost carelessly, like one looking over his shoulder, "Before Abraham was, I AM."

Anyone raising the claims of Jesus is going to be opposed—which is the real reason for the persecution that Mark's Gospel records. As members of the mystical body of Jesus, the Markan disciples are themselves a Messiah provoking others' wrath at the blasphemy of their claim.

Why the Persecution?

IN THE PRECEDING chapter I discussed the salience of persecution in Mark's Gospel, and where it occurred, but I did not address the question, why did the persecution occur? What were its grounds? Joel Marcus suggests that Mark's high Christology was itself the provocation. The Zealots who drove Jesus' followers out of Palestine in the late sixties were violent in their rejection of a Messiah who did not bring worldly rule of the sort they sought. The night-time hearing of Jesus

by the Jewish authorities shows how central was his Messianic claim. In Mark's world, this was a continuing cause of
discord, and not only from those outside the community.
Within the Brotherhood itself there were disciples who fell
away from Jesus' Messianic claims under the pressure of persecution. The disciples described as being rebuked by Jesus in
the Gospel had their counterparts among Mark's people.

This reading of the situation may also explain one of the
characteristics of Mark's Gospel that has often puzzled his
readers—Jesus' repeated injunction to those healed by him
not to reveal the nature of what he has done.[2] He also orders
devils not to reveal his identity. He is keeping a secret. Why?
One of the most influential interpretations of Mark was for-
mulated in the first year of the twentieth century, and it
echoed throughout succeeding years. William Wrede's *The
Messianic Secret* (1901) argued that Jesus was not recognized
as the Messiah in his lifetime. Mark, Wrede argued, made an
attempt to explain this by saying that Jesus *ordered* people to
keep silent on the subject. This was accepted as the best explanation so long as people were still thinking of the Gospels as
an attempt to cope with the biographical facts of Jesus' life.
Now, however, it is more probable that the "secret" reflects
difficulties within the Markan community.

Mark's people have to face the fact that their opponents,
whether Jew or Gentile, do not see what they see—that Jesus
is the Messiah, the Son of God, a divine agent. That is the
source of the persecution. Just as Jesus was plotted against by
his own relatives, driven from Syria on his first visit there,

WHAT THE GOSPELS MEANT

unhonored in his own hometown because he made claims that
were blasphemous, so are his followers in Mark's community
persecuted because they honor those claims. Jesus explains
this mystery in the main parable of Mark's Gospel, the one
that is mysterious because it seems so little mysterious and
Jesus goes to such lengths in order to explain it. The parable,
which he offers as a riddle, runs this way:

> "Hear! See! A sower went out to sow. And it happened as he
> sowed that some seed fell beside the road, and birds came and
> ate it up. And other seed fell on rocky ground, where there
> was little soil, and straightway it shot up because of the thin
> soil, and when the sun rose it was scorched, and it withered
> without root. And other seed fell into a thorn patch, and the
> thorns grew up and strangled it, so it bore no crop. And other
> seed fell on soil that was rich, and it bore a crop that was ris-
> ing and increasing, and they had a yield of thirty times or
> sixty times or a hundred times over." And he said, "Let those
> hear who have ears to hear." (4.3–9)

That last sentence sets the disciples a task, but they have
trouble carrying it out. They are puzzled by the riddle.

> And when he was alone with his close followers and the
> Twelve, they kept worrying at the riddle, and he said to them:
> "The mystery of God's reign is entrusted to you, but to out-
> siders all comes by way of riddles, so that looking they look
> and see not, and listening they listen and hear not, lest they
> turn back and be released." (4.10–12)

40

Then he spells out the meaning of his riddle:

And he says to them: "Do you not understand this riddle?
Then how will you understand the riddles in general? The
sower sows the word. Those beside the road, where the word
is sown, when they hear the word, straightway Satan comes
and takes away the word that was sown in them. And like-
wise those sown on the rocks, when they hear the word, they
straightway take it in with joy, but they lack root and are
shallow, and when they are pressed and persecuted because
of the word, straightway they are trammeled. And others,
sown in the thorn patch, are ones who hear the word, and
their temporal worries and the seduction of wealth and other
kinds of longing enter into them and strangle the word, which
bears no crop. And those sown in soil that is good soil are the
ones who hear the word and take it in and bear a crop thirty
times and sixty times and a hundred times over." (4.13–20)

Scholars have wondered why Jesus makes such a point of
the un-understandability of this "riddle." It seems plain
enough on its face. But modern readers tend to read the passage in terms of individuals—of persons who receive (or do
not receive) the word. Jesus is speaking, here as throughout
the Gospel, in eschatological terms, of the coming of the reign
of heaven, moving to the fulfillment of history. The riddle is
not a story of each soul's reaction to Jesus but an outline of
the entire history of the world. The seeding takes place in
stages, as we can see by the time it takes for the fulfillment
of each one. The first seeds, by the road, are instantly snatched

up by birds. The seeds on rocky land do have a certain development, they first receive the word "with joy" and send down roots, but the roots are not deep enough to withstand persecution. The seeds in the thorn patch go further, and actually send up a crop, but it is choked by worldly desires. Only those in rich soil move through all the stages it takes to produce an abundant and harvestable crop.

What puzzles Mark's people is the fact that God's reign is supposed to have come, with the redemptive death and triumphant Resurrection of Jesus. Why do people still doubt and fight the reign? Jesus is telling them that the advent of the reign is both diachronic and synchronic. The reign is being established, but in some people, even those within the Brotherhood, the word of the reign is still being strangled by thorns, just as those outside the Brotherhood are proving to be stony ground, where no response at all occurs. The Messianic triumph is still hidden—not so much in Jesus' lifetime but in his life as that is being lived out by the members of Mark's gathering. That is the secret message entrusted to the insiders, no matter what outsiders say or think.

A Suffering Messiah

THE REASON THAT Jesus was still not being accepted as Messiah is that he was the *wrong kind* of Messiah. The Messiah was supposed to be a triumphant and regal earthly ruler. When Jesus said that he must be a dying and defeated Messiah, the original followers could not take this in. Peter denied that this could be true—and Jesus called him "Satan," one who throws an obstacle in his leader's path (8.33). This was a further scandal added to the first one. It was bad enough for Jesus to claim to be the Messiah. It is simply insane for him to say that he would suffer death for being the Messiah. This is why Paul called the cross of Jesus "to Jews an affront, to Greeks ignorance" (1 Corinthians 1.23). The call of this Messiah is a call to suffering. Later Christianities will be ruling, crusading, and triumphalist bodies, sitting on papal and imperial thrones, sending out armies to slay the heathen. Its preachers will say that God wants you to be rich, that the Revelation is a path to success. Mark's Gospel could not be further from such distortions of what Jesus said and did and meant. The Messianic community not only suffered because it was *like* Jesus. It suffered because it *was* Jesus.

Mark's Gospel, which set the pattern for future ones, spends a third of its words on the Passion narrative, and it devotes the whole second part of the text to a preparation of the disciples for the "affront" of the cross. It thus has the simplest structure of all the Gospels. The first half is spent in the northern part of Palestine, mainly around Galilee, announcing the reign of heaven, casting out devils, and healing. The mood darkens as Jesus moves south into Judaea and toward Jerusalem (his only visit there in Mark) and predicts, three times over, that he must suffer and die in order to rise. The disciples cannot accept these predictions.

Raymond Brown argues that John's Gospel is probably closer to history when it shows Jesus going up to Jerusalem every year, not just at the end of his life (3B 52). But Mark's Gospel sets the tone of the others by aiming everything toward the earliest statement of Jesus' Revelation, quoted by Paul—"that Messiah died for our sins, in accord with the Sacred Writings" (1 Corinthians 15.3–4). Mark has that climax always in mind, as befits a community that is reliving the Passion of Jesus while it ponders and prays over it. Chesterton captured well the dramatic shape of the Synoptics:

> It is a story that begins in the paradise of Galilee, a pastoral and peaceful land having really some hint of Eden, and gradually climbs the rising country into the mountains that are nearer to the storm-clouds and the stars, as to a mountain of Purgatory. He may be met as if straying in strange places, or stopped on the way for discussion or dispute, but his face is set toward the mountain city. That is the meaning of that great culmination when he crested the ridge and stood at the turning of the road and suddenly cried aloud, lamenting over Jerusalem.

NOTES

1. Compare the land flowing with milk and honey (Exodus 3.8), the river flowing with honey (Job 20.17), the excessive bread from heaven (Exodus 16.4), the trees bearing fruit in every month (Ezekiel 47.12). the overflowing cup (Psalm 23.5).

2. When Matthew and Luke use material from Mark, they usually omit the injunction to secrecy—see their treatment of Mk 1.34, 3.11–12, 5.43, 7.17, 24, 36, 0.28–31, 13.3.

3. Mark's Artistry

MARK'S CONSTANT though implicit reference to the Sacred Writings of the Jews can make one wonder: was Mark himself a profound scholar of the Hebrew Scripture? But we should not think of Mark as some individual genius. He is able to draw on the joint reflections that believing Brothers and Sisters engaged in at the gatherings. They pondered the way Jesus chided the disciples for not understanding his place in Jewish history and destiny. They had initially continued their worship in the synagogues, where they tried to fit the Revelation of Jesus into the texts and services of those religious houses, using the only Bible they knew and accepted—as we can see Paul doing in his treatment of the Sacred Writings.

When they formed their separate gatherings, they continued this practice, producing the early hymns, baptismal formulas, and creedal statements to be found in Paul—all of them heavy with Scriptural language. We have seen these sessions represented symbolically in Luke's story of the two travelers to Emmaus, where Jesus explains himself out of the Sacred Writings. Many scholars now believe that Mark's text had a liturgical use, that appropriate parts of it were read as the community celebrated baptisms, the Passion, the Resurrection—probably in conjunction with the relevant parts of Jewish Scripture, the same practice that would be observed in later church liturgies (4B 51).

Were the gatherings, then, just making up the story of Jesus as they read their Jewish Bible? But the words would not have had any force unless they were being applied to what they knew and remembered about Jesus, what was accepted in the larger community. Traditions Paul was careful to hand on were guarded and pondered by other disciples. Mark himself makes the contact with actual events real for those in his community who knew of them, including the sons of Simon of Cyrene and the naked boy who ran out of the garden of Gethsemane. Raymond Brown's words are worth repeated pondering:

> There was no massive Christian indifference as to what actually happened at the end of Jesus' life; the Passion Narratives were not simply made up out of Scripture; there was a core of memory that governed the shaping of the tradition, and we have traces of that memory in the kerygmatic formulas of the pre-Gospel period. (4B 51–52)

But if we grant that there were real memories of Jesus' life being explained in the light of Scripture, that raises problems about the Gospel's sources for such memories. What, for instance, of events that no disciple witnessed? Where did information about such events come from? When Jesus prayed in Gethsemane, his disciples were asleep. How do we know what he said? When he was questioned by Caiaphas or Pilate, none of his followers was there. Yet we have verbatim interchanges recorded.

Let us begin with Gethsemane. There was an independent tradition that Jesus had prayed to avoid death—not a thing Christians would be likely to make up. We get evidence of that tradition in the Letter to the Hebrews 5.7–10:

> In the days of his flesh, praying and pleading to the one who could rescue him from death, with outpoured loud outcry and tears, and answered because of his humility, even though he was Son, he learned how to submit from what he underwent, and, completed in this way, he was the source of continuing rescue to all who heed him, hailed by God as a high priest in the line of Melchisedech.

This passage and the Gospel accounts fit the primitive tradition in the hymn Paul reports in the Epistle to the Philippians, that Jesus was "so *submissive* as to die, by death on a cross" (2.8, emphasis added).

Mark knows the opening of Jesus' prayer in the garden, *Abba,* the Aramaic for "Father," which he translates into Greek for his readers. When Mark quotes Jesus using his original language, he is close enough to his sources to be giving the Lord's *ipsissima verba.* He does it here, at the beginning of the Passion, as he will at the end, when he quotes the Aramaized Hebrew of Psalm 22, *Eli, Eli, lama sabachthani,* "My God, my God, why have you deserted me?"[1]

But what of the words Jesus spoke while the disciples were asleep? The faithful thought of Jesus as reliving the abandonment of the chosen people, so they reflected on the suffering servant of God in the Psalms and Isaiah and in the ordeal of his Davidic precursor. When Jesus goes up the Mount of Olives, he repeats David's ascent of the same mount, with weeping followers, to face the fact that he has been betrayed by his son Absalom and the son's associate Ahitophel (2 Samuel 15.30–31). The Brothers would remember that Ahitophel later hanged himself (2 Samuel 17.23), one of only two people to do that in the Bible. The other one is the betrayer Judas (4B 125).

Before his prayer, Jesus tells the three called to be with him, "My soul is deep in misery" *(perilypos)*, recalling Psalm 42.6, "How deep I am sunk in misery" *(perilypos)*—a psalm John also uses in connection with Jesus' Passion, suggesting early Christian use of it in this context (4B 154). Jesus' words in the garden have the main elements of the Lord's Prayer in Matthew and Luke, a prayer that may have been formed from Mark's account of the agony in the garden. Jesus begins with "Father," and prays that "your design be fulfilled" (the exact words of the third petition in the Lord's Prayer), and asks that the followers be spared "the final Test" *(Peirasmos)*, which is the sixth petition of the Lord's Prayer. Christians pray along with Jesus in his anguished address to the Father in Gethsemane.

The exchanges with Caiaphas and Pilate are more easily explained, since the Jewish charge against Jesus is the same that Mark's followers heard from the Jews of their day, that Jesus falsely claimed to be the Messiah. The accusation of Pilate was clear from the public sentence of Jesus' death for being the putative king of the Jews. That was the charge affixed to the cross. Jesus' cry of abandonment from the cross was taken from Psalm 22, a psalm around which the Brothers and Sisters organized their meditations on the Passion and death of Jesus.

Intercalations

THE DEPTH OF biblical reflection on each separate incident of the Lord's sayings was not produced by Mark alone. He obviously draws from a communal treasury of memories prayed over, taught, shared in the gatherings, given form in an oral culture. The separate units of these traditions are called by the scholars pericopes (Greek for "rounded segments"), and we see the different ways they can be used by comparing Matthew's and Luke's treatment of material from Mark. Did Mark simply collect what he wanted from the prayerful readings of the Sacred Writings that preceded him? After all, he does not embark on such obviously creative exercises as Matthew and Luke did in their treatment of Jesus' birth.

Yet there is artistry in Mark's shaping of his story. We can see that when he arranges a sequence of several pericopes on the Exodus theme. Another Markan practice is to interrupt a story, inserting a different event before resuming the story. Scholars call these insertions intercalations. They have also been called a "sandwiching" technique or "bookends" or "inclusions." The inserted material interacts with the surrounding tale, giving it new depths of reference. Here are some examples of the technique.

VERSES 2.1–12

A crowd breaks through the roof of a building where Jesus is jammed in among a throng, bringing him a paralytic for healing. Jesus tells the man his trust is rewarded, and he forgives his sins. The conversation with the man is broken by some scribes, who call it blasphemous for Jesus to claim he can forgive sins. Jesus reads their thoughts and asks which is easier, to forgive sins or to heal paralytic limbs. The story then resumes with his physical healing of the man. The tie between spiritual and physical health is emphasized by the collocation of the stories, and the eschatological reign of heaven is proclaimed.

VERSES 3.20–35

Word that Jesus is healing the possessed leads some, including his own family, to think he must be working prodigies by diabolical powers of his own. "Hearing these things, his relatives went forward to overpower him, for they said, 'He is mad.'" The story breaks off here for Jesus to defend himself from the idea that he is a madman, or that he heals the possessed by the power of the devil. Why, Jesus asks, would the devil fight devils? "If a reign is divided against itself, how can that reign survive? And if house members are divided against themselves, how can that house survive?" He says that evil

elements in the reign of worldly power all work in conjunction to hold history in their grip. His own coming reign must
be just as firm in its unity—which is why the relatives who
do not believe in him have been left outside. Their story is
picked up again when Jesus' disciples say, "See! Your mother
and your brothers outdoors are seeking you." But he says that
his followers are his real relatives. He has forged a new human
community, extending it out from the chosen people.

VERSES 5.21–43

The story of Jairus, a leader of the synagogue, is broken
off after Jairus has asked Jesus to come heal his daughter, who
is ill and close to death. Despite this air of crisis, Jesus is dis-
tracted by a woman with a perpetual menstrual flow, making
her unclean and incapable of normal human contacts or Temple observance. She defies the taboo on unclean contacts by
silently making her way through the crowd and touching
Jesus' garment. He says that her trust surmounts all the difficulties of her situation, and she is healed. This outcast from
the synagogue pushes in before Jesus can help the prominent
synagogue official. After healing her, Jesus is ready to go on
to the house of Jairus—but now he is told that the daughter
has, in the interim, died. Jesus has been summoned in vain.
But he tells Jairus to maintain his trust—Jesus has to instruct
this synagogue official, where the woman had persisted without instruction. The different responses from the ritually pure
and the ritually impure are emphasized here, as in much of
the Gospel, where Jesus breaks through the barriers fencing
off the "unclean."

VERSES 6.7–44

Jesus sends his followers off on a first mission of their own, and before they can report back to him, the news of their missionary activity spreads—it reaches Herod, who fears that John the Baptist has risen again to challenge his rule. This is the cue for Mark to create a flashback telling how Herod killed John. After this digression, the disciples come back with good reports of their mission, and this leads into the feeding of the five thousand, the first parts of the Exodus sequence discussed earlier. Mark has shown the succession of Jesus to his precursor, who was an Elisha to the Messianic revelation.

VERSES 11.12–25

On his way to Jerusalem, Jesus curses a fig tree that provides no fruit, saying, "Let no one, ever, from this time forward, eat fruit of yours." He and the disciples go on to the Temple, the fig tree apparently forgotten in the story. This is the crucial moment in Mark's Gospel, when Jesus declares the end of the sacrificial system of Temple worship. This culminates the denunciations of prophet after prophet. The words of 1 Samuel 15.22 were: "Obedience is better than sacrifice, and to listen to God is better than the fat of rams." Hosea had said, "Loyalty is my desire, not sacrifice, not whole-offerings but the knowledge of God." And Psalm 51.16–17:

> You have no delight in sacrifice,
> if I brought thee an offering, thou wouldst not accept it.
> My sacrifice, O God, is a broken spirit,
> a wounded heart. O God, thou wilt not despise.

So Jesus drives out the merchants changing profane coin (Roman denarii with the "divine" emperor's image) to "clean" shekels that can buy animals for sacrifice in the Temple. He quotes Isaiah 56.7 as he disrupts the sacrifice: "Was it not written, 'My house shall be known as a house of prayer for all peoples?'" He says that the merchants have turned God's house into a robbers' cave, referring to Jeremiah 7.10–11: "You come and stand before me in this house, which bears my name, and say, 'We are safe!'—safe, you think, to indulge in all these abominations. Do you think that this house, this house that bears my name, is a robbers' cave?"

This action is, in Mark's Gospel, the real cause of Jesus' death—the Temple authorities will not stand the blasphemous treatment of their Temple rites, and the Roman authorities will see in this a revolutionary disruption of Jewish stability. The religious affront will be read as a political act. But now Mark returns to the fig tree. When the disciples go out of Jerusalem, they find the fig tree blasted and lifeless. This fulfills another prophecy of Jeremiah (8.13):

I would gather their harvest, says the Lord,
    but there are no grapes on the vine,
no figs on the fig tree,
    even their leaves are withered.

When the disciples marvel at the power of Jesus' curse on the fig tree, he tells them: "In truth I tell you that if someone says to this mountain [the Temple Mount], 'Rise from your place and be flung into the sea,' not doubting in his heart but believing that what he says is done, so it will be for him." This whole sequence is a condemnation of the Temple cult as currently practiced, and a prediction of its fall.

VERSES 14.54–72

The betrayal by Peter is wrapped around the account of Jesus' trial in the high priest's house. "And Peter followed from a long way behind so far as inside the courtyard of the high priest, and he was sitting with the servants as he kept warm by the fire." There we leave Peter while we learn how, upstairs in the house, Jesus is condemned and beaten. Then we switch back out to the courtyard. "And while Peter was still below in the courtyard, one of the high priest's serving women saw Peter keeping warm, and peering at him closely she says: 'You too were with the man from Nazareth, this Jesus.'" This whole passage was very meaningful to Mark's community, which had known defectors and those who denied the Messianic claims of Jesus. The great details spelt out here may have had recognizable parallels to what was occurring under persecution in Mark's original audience.

> But he denied it, saying: "I know nothing, nor do I understand what you are saying." And he went outside into the forecourt, and the maid, seeing him again, began to tell the bystanders that "this man is one of them." But he again denied it. And a little later the bystanders were saying to Peter: "Certainly you are of their company, for of course you are a Galilean." But he began to curse and swear that "I know no such man as you are talking about." And the cock gave a

second crow. And Peter called to mind the word Jesus had
spoken to him. "Before the cock's second crow, you will three
times deny me." And he broke down into tears.

The Gospel Ending

THE END OF the Gospel also had some special meaning for
Mark's persecuted community. In the best attested manuscript
tradition, Mark gives no account of appearances by the risen
Jesus. It has been said that he did not know of any such appearances; but that cannot be true, since Mark has Jesus predict at
the Last Supper his appearances to the disciples: "After I am
raised, I shall go before you into Galilee" (14.28). And the
angel tells the women who find the empty tomb: "Do not be
astounded. You are seeking Jesus, the one from Nazareth who
was crucified. He has been raised, he is not here. Look!—the
place where they laid him. But hurry, tell his disciples and
Peter that he is going before you into Galilee. There you will
see him, as he told you" (16.6–7).

In the Gospel's stark final sentence, the women simply dis-
obey the angel. They are too frightened to proclaim the risen
Messiah: "But the women went off and fled from the tomb,
for panic and terror possessed them, and they said nothing to
anyone, for they were afraid." This was a shockingly abrupt
ending for some later Christians, so they created a "softer
landing" for the Gospel—in two increments.[2] These are not
in Mark's manner, and they are obvious face-savers. There is
a shorter addition (verse 8b), in which the women obey the
angel and deliver his message to Peter and the others. Then

there is another addition (verses 9–14), of appearances cobbled together from the Gospels of Luke and John (written, remember, after Mark). There, in verse 18, is a reference to fearless snake handling that will come back to haunt American Fundamentalists.

None of this is in the best manuscripts. Again, Mark has written something with specific reference to his audience—something too cryptic or embarrassing for others to deal with. Mark is clearly referring to a scandal in his own community, where women renounced the Messiah out of fear. The persecution against which Mark is bracing his fellows has taken its toll. Mark will not sweeten the story, even as he signals that Jesus awaits his followers in their own Galilee of the mind.

NOTES

1. Mark quotes Jesus using Aramaic in two other places, *Talitha koum* (5.41), "Get up, child," and *Ephphatha* (7.34), "Be opened."

2. A third addition was found for the Gospel when a fifth-century papyrus found in the nineteenth century (called the Freer logion from its possession by the Freer Library in Washington). It adds an extenuation of Jesus' rebuke to the disciples for their unbelief.

II. MATTHEW

Report from the Teaching Body of Jesus

OF THE THREE *Synoptic Gospels, the later two—Matthew and Luke, which both use the first one—must have been written long enough after Mark for his Gospel to have spread and been in general use outside the original community for which it was written. This means that both Matthew and Luke wrote after the destruction of the Temple (70 CE), which followed quickly on Mark's composition. Developments in the gatherings, reflected in the later two Gospels, indicate that a decade at the very least must intervene between them and Mark. A latest possible date for Matthew is set by the letters of Ignatius of Antioch and the Didache (thought to have come from the years around 100–110 CE), since both show knowledge of Matthew. That would put Matthew's Gospel in the eighties or nineties CE, and more toward the end of that span than near its beginning.*

Since Matthew and Luke share some pericopes not in Mark, they are said to have two sources ("the two source theory"). This shared non-Markan material is concentrated on sayings of Jesus, not his acts, and the presumed collection of sayings is called "Q" (for the German word Quelle,

"Source"). Attempts to re-create this collection of sayings are highly speculative, and they are complicated by the fact that Matthew and Luke seem each to have his own third source, called, respectively, "M" and "L." A consideration of all these factors is what is known as "the Synoptic problem." Though Matthew and Luke both knew Mark and Q, they did not know each other. They drew on their separate sources—for instance, in writing entirely different versions of the genealogy and birth of Jesus. That may indicate that they wrote at about the same time but in separate locales.

Matthew's Gospel shows that the community in and for which he wrote had taken on more formal procedures and structures than were known by Paul or Mark. Peter is now said (16.18) to be the stone on which the gathering is built up (though Matthew continues the tradition of criticizing Peter for his denial of the Lord).[1] Matthew is a great tidier-upper. He collects the sayings of Jesus in five large discourses, each organized around a separate theme and spaced out to call for separate consideration. These have a didactic purpose. The actions of Jesus are distributed to lead up to or follow from individual discourses (the most famous of them being the first, called the Sermon on the Mount).

Matthew is also meticulous in citing specific parts of the Sacred Writings that are relevant to Jesus' acts.[2] These are appended to events in a loose way, as opposed to being deeply interwoven into events, without specific citation, which was Mark's practice. The emphasis on biblical specificity has made many believe that Matthew was a Jewish believer in Jesus. It used to be claimed, in fact, that he either wrote or translated an earlier version of a Gospel in Aramaic. But John Meier argues that Matthew is ignorant of certain things any Jew, at least any Palestinian Jew, would have known. Matthew believes, for instance, that Pharisees and Sadducees were united, though in fact they were deeply divided. And Matthew misreads the prophet Zechariah in an amateurish way.[3] Meier concludes that Matthew was an educated Gentile who studied Jewish Scripture, as all early Brothers and Sisters were expected to do.

Where and for whom did Matthew write? A broad consensus looks to Antioch, known in Paul's time as a place of mixed Jewish and Gentile Brothers and Sisters, a place where Peter's role was important and contentious, and where Ignatius and the Didache, the earliest authors to cite Matthew, also originated. Antioch, moreover, was a city developed enough to have a school of Christian training—and some conclude that the systematic, didactic, and even pedantic nature of the Gospel was used for teaching and learning in such a school.[4] Whether the schooling was formal or informal, this Gospel seems peculiarly fitted for such use.

NOTES

1. Arlo J. Nau, *Peter in Matthew: Discipleship, Diplomacy, and Dispraise, with an Assessment of Power and Privilege in the Petrine Office* (Liturgical Press, 1992).

2. There are eleven of the "formula citations" (as they are called) accepted as certain by most scholars. See Krister Stendahl, *The School of St. Matthew and Its Use of the Old Testament*, 2nd ed. (Gleerup, 1968), pp. 97–127.

3. John P. Meier, *The Vision of Matthew: Christ, Church, and Morality*

in the First Gospel (Paulist Press, 1979), pp. 18–24. Matthew says that Jesus'
entry into Jerusalem riding an animal "fulfills" a prophecy of Zechariah 9.9:

> Your king is coming . . .
> humble and mounted on an ass,
> on a foal, the young of a she-ass.

By the laws of Hebrew parallelism, that third line is simply an expanded
repetition of the second, so only one animal is referred to. But Matthew took
the lines as referring to two animals. He makes Jesus tell his followers to find
"a donkey tethered and a foal beside her" (21.2), then he makes Jesus some-
how ride *both* the animals into Jerusalem (21.7).

4. Stendahl, op. cit., pp. 20–29.

4. Birth Narrative

ONE OF THE many signs that Matthew and Luke did not know each other's work is that they produced such different accounts of the birth of Jesus.[1] Taken together by later readers, these two Gospels created the wonderful iconography of Christmas. But they contribute clashing elements to the scene. Matthew gives us the flight into Egypt, the slaughter of the innocents, and the Magi. Luke gives us rejection at an inn, the angels and shepherds, and the presentation in the Temple. Neither one can be relying on eyewitnesses—how could the evangelists know what Joseph was dreaming, or Herod was scheming, or Simeon was singing? A naïve early attempt to save the historicity of the narratives was to assume that Joseph and Mary had told the evangelists' sources what happened. According to this theory, Joseph must be the source for Matthew's Gospel, in which he plays the leading role, and Mary must be Luke's ultimate source.

The trouble with this view is that the two stories are contradictory. "As a wag has suggested, that theory presupposes that Mary and Joseph never spoke to each other" (1B 525). Besides, if family tradition, in some form, is supposed to be the authenticator of the narratives, why did Jesus' family doubt his mission and identity (Mk 3.12, 3.13, Jn 7.5)? If relatives had known the miraculous nature of his origin, they would have been his enthusiastic supporters, not his critics and foes.

A documentary approach to the birth narratives makes no sense. As was earlier noted, the Gospels are built "backward" from the basic Kerygma, as Paul reported it, that "Messiah died for our sins, in accord with the Sacred Writings, that he was buried, that he arose on the third day, in accord with the Sacred Writings." That is the basic meaning of Jesus. The evangelists preface this with oral accounts that have accumulated from Jesus' earthly ministry, dating that public ministry back to Jesus' baptism by John. Matthew and Luke preface that with the Messianic signs of Jesus' birth, presenting symbolically the meaning of Jesus' appearance among humans. They show the event in a blaze of scriptural signs.

In this way, the birth narratives make up "bookends" with the Passion and Resurrection narratives. The birth narratives look both ways, backward to foreshadowings in Jewish history, and forward to the climax of the Jesus story. Motifs from the Passion and Resurrection are seen as present from the beginning—the opening toward the Gentiles (Magi at the beginning, the centurion at the end), the suffering of innocents (children at the beginning, Jesus at the end), unwilling testimony from foes (Herod at the beginning, Pilate at the end), portents in a dream (first Joseph's, then that of Pilate's wife).

The differences in the two birth narratives come from the

different aspects of Jesus' complex role that each evangelist chose to emphasize. Matthew focuses on the kingly (Mosaic and Davidic) role of the Messiah, centered around Joseph's status as a Davidid (descendant of David) and Jesus' travel to and from Egypt in an Exodus pattern. Luke stresses the priestly line of the Baptist's father and the Temple observance of all those who welcome Jesus into life (Zechariah, Elizabeth, Simeon, Anna). Augustine recognized these different functions of the genealogies and birth accounts, Matthew showing Jesus as king, Luke showing him as priest.[2] Matthew traces the genealogy of Jesus from Abraham, in kingly line through David. Luke traces it up to God himself, in priestly line. This is a way of separately highlighting what was joined in the primitive Kerygma as Paul reported it: "the revelation of His [God's] son, born *of David's seed* according to the flesh, but marked out in might as *God's son* according to the Spirit of holiness at his resurrection from the dead—Jesus Messiah, our Lord" (Romans 1.3). The union of flesh and divinity, of David and the Spirit, lies behind the two narratives.

One year I sent out a Christmas card quoting one of Augustine's Christmas sermons (Number 191). Since Augustine referred in the passage to Jesus' suffering and death, a close friend told me it was inappropriate to mention such things at a time of good cheer and Christmas rejoicing. But the Gospel birth narratives are far from feel-good stories. They tell of a family outcast and exiled, hunted and rejected. They tell of children killed, of a sword to pierce the mother's heart, of a judgment on the nations. The point of the story lies in the contrast between heavenly alertness and earthly dullness. The

Messiah is a rejected Messiah from the very outset. Here is the passage in which Augustine traced the true meaning of Christmas:

> Man's maker was made man that he, Ruler of the Milky Way, might nurse at his mother's breasts; that the Bread might hunger, the Fountain thirst, the Light sleep, the Way be tired in journey; that Truth might be accused by false witness, the Teacher be beaten with whips, the Foundation be suspended on wood; that Strength might weaken, that the Healer might be wounded, that Life might die.

The Genealogy

GIVEN THE symbolic significance of the whole birth narrative, the genealogy will not offer the kind of evidence that a birth certificate must verify. The lineage is more heraldic, to indicate the kind of heritage that can produce the heroic nature of its bearer. "The genealogy is not a record of man's biological productivity, but a demonstration of God's providence" (1B 68). The artificial arrangement of the generations in Matthew—three groups of fourteen ancestors—is meant as a shorthand history of the whole Jewish people, leading to its fulfillment in Jesus. The neat divisions confirm that Matthew is writing for schoolroom presentation. According to this schematic (and mnemonic) history, "exactly fourteen biological generations separated such crucial moments in salvation history as the call of Abraham, the accession of David, the Babylonian exile, and the coming of the Messiah" (1B 74).

The most interesting things about Matthew's genealogy are (1) the large and unusual role played by descent through a woman, and (2) the fact that the four women chosen to play such a leading part were all of an ambiguous status. To put it more bluntly, they were not types that proper Victorians would boast of in their bloodline. They are

1. Tamar, a pretended prostitute who seduces her father-in-law (Genesis 38.15–25)
2. Rahab, an actual prostitute (Joshua 2.1)
3. Ruth, a Moabite (Ruth 1.4) and therefore "unclean"
4. Bathsheba, the object of David's adultery (2 Samuel 11.4)

Though these women were not all sinners, there was something improper in their history—yet good came from each of their couplings. Tamar continued Judah's line, Rahab helped Israel reach the Promised Land, Ruth aided in the conquest of Jericho, and Bathsheba bore Solomon, the son of David.

In post-biblical Jewish piety, these extraordinary unions and initiatives were seen as the work of the Holy Spirit. These women were held up as examples of how God uses the unexpected to triumph over human obstacles and intervenes on behalf of his planned Messiah. It is the combination of the scandalous or irregular unions and of divine intervention through the women that explains Matthew's choice in the genealogy. . . . It was to Matthew's interest that the four Old Testament women were also Gentiles or associated with Gentiles (Uriah's wife). (1B 73–74)

Tamar was a Canaanite (or perhaps an Aramean), Rahab was a Canaanite, Ruth was a Moabite, and Bathsheba was married to a Hittite—so she is referred to in the genealogy not by her own name, but as " the wife of Uriah," to keep the Gentile common denominator to the fore.

Matthew has subtly underlined the importance of Mary in the conception of Jesus. Not only is she a woman through whom the Davidic line is extended, but she is an "irregular" heir to David, through Joseph, who acknowledges Jesus as his son. Brown thinks that Matthew may even be addressing an early form of the later charge that Jesus was a bastard (1B 527, 534–42).

Even the more normal descent through the males is irregular in Matthew's list. Brown suggests that this is done to include representatives of all twelve tribes, since the Messiah would restore them all—a fact that Jesus affirms in his choice of the Twelve to follow him (Mt. 19.28).

> Jesus is Abraham's son not through the older Ishmael but through Isaac. Jesus is Isaac's son not through the first-born Esau but through Jacob. Among the twelve sons of Jacob, it is from Judah, the fourth son, that Jesus is derived, for to Judah was promised the eternal scepter. Yet the brothers of Judah are not forgotten by Matthew, since Jesus is related to the whole of Israel. (1B 69)

But was Jesus in fact born from David's line? That was a royal line, and there is nothing royal about the circumstances of Jesus' upbringing.

If Joseph and Jesus were Davidids, they must have belonged to a lateral branch of the family rather than to the direct royal lineage. There is not the slightest indication in the accounts of the ministry of Jesus that his family was of ancestral nobility or royalty. If Jesus were a dauphin, there would have been none of the wonderment about his pretensions. He appears in the Gospels as a man of unimpressive background from an unimportant village. (1B 88)

Yet Brown, like a majority of New Testament scholars, believes that Jesus was in fact descended from David, albeit by an obscure branch. A claim to the relationship is very early, already accepted by the fifties CE (Romans 1.3), and not challenged by Jesus' relatives, who were critical of him on other grounds. Paul's word is sufficient on this point.

Paul knew the Palestinian situation, and was always sensitive to correction from Jerusalem. Would he have used it [the Davidic lineage] if he knew that Jesus was not really descended from David? Would this not have left him vulnerable to the Jerusalem following of James or to those who were questioning his apostolate precisely on the grounds that he knew little of the earthly Jesus? Scholars who tell us that Paul may never have inquired about Jesus' ancestry forget that to a man with Paul's training as a Pharisee, the Davidic ancestry of the Messiah would be a question of paramount importance, especially in the period before his conversion when he was seeking arguments to refute the followers of Jesus. Paul, who twice insists on his own Benjamite descent, would scarcely

have been disinterested in the Davidic descent of Jesus.
(1B 508)

Matthew seems to have based his entire genealogy on this historical fact of Jesus' Davidic descent. The very organization of ancestors into three groups of fourteen is probably based on the name of David. Earlier attempts to say that fourteen is twice seven, the number of the Creation, have not won much acceptance, since there is no convincing reason to double the number. But the common Jewish practice of *gematria* (number symbolism in a name, as at Revelation 13.18) is widely accepted as the basis of the genealogy's shape. By the rules of *gematria*, "David" has three consonants in Hebrew, and their numerical value adds up to fourteen—whence the three sets of fourteen names in the genealogy. Besides, David's name is the fourteenth in Matthew's list.

> In a genealogy of 3 x 14, the one name with three consonants and a value of fourteen is also placed in the fourteenth spot. When one adds that this name is mentioned immediately before the genealogy and twice at its conclusion, and that it is honored by the title King, coincidence becomes effectively ruled out. The name David is the key to the pattern of Matthew's genealogy.[3]

Virginal Conception

"VIRGIN BIRTH," the unfortunate common term, is a misnomer for what Matthew and Luke describe—a virginal conception. Matthew says that this conception is a fulfillment of Isaiah 7.14, which reads in the Hebrew: "A *young woman* is with child, and she will bear a son, and will call him Immanuel." Matthew, however, says that a virgin *(parthenos)* will give birth, since he is relying on the Greek (Septuagint) translation of Isaiah. It has often been argued that Matthew accepted (consciously or unconsciously) the Septuagint "mistranslation" in order to prove the virginal conception of Jesus. But Brown argues that this is all a tangle of misperceptions—muddling the meanings of Jewish "prophecy," of Matthew's understanding of "fulfillment," and of the original sense of Isaiah 7.14.

The situation at Isaiah 7 was this: the prophet was threatening the wicked King Ahaz with the birth from a particular woman of a son in David's line who would deliver Judah from its enemies. The "young woman" must be a recognizable person for the threat to have force, and the Septuagint did not really change the meaning since she is still a young virgin when the threat is issued. Matthew is saying that God wrought wonders for David's line in the past, and Jesus is the inheritor of all these symbols of the Jewish people's deliverance.

> In summary, the Masoritic [Hebrew] text of Isaiah 7.14 does not refer to a virginal conception in the distant future. The sign offered by the prophet was the imminent [eighth century BCE] birth of a child, probably Davidic, but naturally conceived, who would illustrate God's providential care for his people. The child would help to preserve the House of

David and would thus signify that God was still "with us" [Immanuel]. (IB 148)

The virginal conception of Jesus is not a gynecological or obstetric teaching, but a theological one, as defined by the Gospel of John 1.12–13: "As many as accepted him [Jesus], to those who trust in his title, who are born not of bloodline nor from flesh's desire, nor man's design, but from God." This emphasis on God's intervention for his chosen ones signals, in the case of Jesus, a new beginning, a fresh creation, a point made when Matthew called the genealogy of Jesus "a book of his origin" *(genesis)*. For many years, the Catholic church tried to defend the idea of Mary's perpetual virginity by denying what the Gospels unhesitatingly declare, that Jesus had brothers. The brothers were called cousins by Catholic exegetes, even though the Greek language has very clear and detailed terms for all blood relationships. Even Catholic exegetes now agree, with the Jesuit Joseph Fitzmyer, that "the affirmation of Mary's virginity . . . is never presented in any biological sense."[4] Raymond Brown rightly cautions:

All Christians should be wary of any implication that the conception of Jesus in wedlock would detract from his nobility or Mary's sanctity. In its origin, the virginal conception shows no traces whatsoever of an anti-sexual bias and should not be made to support one. For the evangelists it was a visible sign of God's gracious intervention in connection with the becoming of his Son; in no way did that intervention make ordinary conception in marriage less holy. (1B 530)

Joseph and Egypt

THE ANNUNCIATION of a child who will be important in God's plan for the Jews is often made by an angel in the Sacred Writings—as with Ishmael (Genesis 16.7–12) and with Samson (Judges 13.3) or it is announced by God himself, as with Isaac (Genesis 17.15–16). It is accomplished in a dream for Joseph, since his name and the connection with Egypt recall the patriarch Joseph, an expert interpreter of dreams who was taken to Egypt, where he deciphered Pharaoh's dreams (Genesis 37.19, 41.25). Matthew's Joseph is instructed in dreams on four occasions (1.20, 2.13, 2.19, 2.22). He is first informed that Mary's child is begotten by the Holy Spirit. Then, once the child is born, dreams tell Joseph how to protect it. The angel first tells him he must take Jesus to Egypt, in order to escape Herod's hunt for the new Jewish king, just as the infant Moses had to escape from the murderous Pharaoh. Brown traces the parallels (1B 113):

Mt 2.13–14   Herod was going to search for the child to destroy, so Joseph took the child and his mother and went away.

Exodus 2.15   Pharaoh sought to do away with Moses, so Moses went away.

Mt 2.16   Herod went to Bethlehem and massacred all the boys of two years of age and under.

Exodus 1.22   Pharaoh commanded that every male born to the Hebrews be cast into the Nile.

Mt 2.19   Herod died.

WHAT THE GOSPELS MEANT

Exodus 2.23	The king of Egypt died.
Mt 2.19–20	The angel of the Lord said to Joseph in Egypt: "Go back to the land of Israel, for those who were seeking the child's life are dead."
Exodus 4.19	The Lord said to Moses in Midian: "Return to Egypt, for all those who were seeking your life are dead."
Mt 2.21	Joseph took the child and his mother and went back to the land of Israel.
Exodus 4.20	Moses took along his wife and his children and returned to Egypt.

In both cases, God is protecting the person with a special mission.

Magi

THE MAGI symbolize the future ingathering of Gentiles to the Jewish Messiah. This is an eschatological sign, as in Isaiah 60.3, 6:

> And the nations shall march towards your light,
>   and their kings to your sunrise. . . .
> Camels in droves shall cover the land,
>   dromedaries of Midian and Ephah,
> all coming from Sheba
>   laden with golden spice and frankincense.

Or in Psalm 72.10:

The kings of Tarshish and the islands shall bring gifts,
the kings of Sheba and Seba shall present their tribute.

Though the general theme of Gentiles bringing gifts is part
of the Messianic scenario, the Magi in Matthew are not kings
(nor are they specified as three). They are seers and diviners,
patterned on Balaam, a Gentile from the East, who is expert
in spells (Numbers 22.7). Asked by King Balak to curse the
Jewish people, Balaam is led by God to bless them instead,
with a prophecy (Numbers 24.17):

A star shall come forth out of Jacob,
A comet arise from Israel.

Pre-existing Traditions

BROWN CONTENDS that the elements of the birth narrative
were not invented by Matthew but are used by him. The fact
that the Joseph story and the Magi story were originally separate traditions can be seen from the clumsy way Matthew
combines them. The Magi have a star to guide them. Why do
they stop off and ask for guidance from Herod? This is done
simply to tie in the Magi to the slaughter of the young, which
comes from the Egyptian tale.

Herod's failure to find the child at Bethlehem would be perfectly intelligible in a story in which there were no Magi
who come from the East and where he had only general scriptural knowledge about Bethlehem to guide him. It becomes

ludicrous when the way to the house has been pointed out
by a star which comes to rest over it, and when the path to
the door of the house in a small village has been blazed by
exotic foreigners. (1B 191)

But this clumsy narrative structure has a symbolic significance. It is fitting that the Gentile Magi seek the child by the
light of pagan knowledge but can reach him only by learning
of the importance of Bethlehem from the Sacred Writings.
Future Gentiles will be brought to Jesus when they accept the
Jewish promise of the Messiah.

Where did Matthew find the components for his narrative?
Brown notes that Joseph's dreams, the wandering Magi, the
evil king are folkloric in nature. He compares them to the
mystery plays of the Middle Ages, which gave popular drama
to scriptural elements. Scripture supplied the basic materials
for stories with creative immediacy—Joseph the patriarch,
Balaam's prophecy, Rachel's lament, the pharaoh. Drawing a
parallel between Pharaoh and Herod would have come naturally to those who remembered the cruelties of the latter—
how he had three of his own children put to death, and ordered
his soldiers to kill political prisoners when he died—"so shall
all Judaea and every household weep for me" (1B 226-27)—
calling up echoes of Rachel's outcry over her lost children (Mt
2.18). Matthew's aim was to link these pious reflections to the
broader themes of the Kerygma as part of the Messiah's Jewish background. Brown rightly brought out the essential point
when he called his book on Matthew's and Luke's accounts
The Birth of the Messiah.

NOTES

1. The normal term for Matthew's and Luke's accounts of Jesus' origin is "infancy narratives," but Raymond Brown rightly calls this a misnomer. The evangelists tell the story of Jesus' conception and birth, not of his infancy. Apocryphal stories of Jesus as a boy are outside the canon and have no historic or theological worth.

2. Augustine, *The Consistency of the Gospel Writers*, 1.4–5.

3. W. D. Davies and Dale C. Allison, *The Gospel According to Saint Matthew* (T. & T. Clark, 1988), vol. 1, p. 165. See also. p. 165. n. 20:

That the meaning of Matthew's fourteen lies in David's name is supported by this fact: although the Chronicler counted fourteen Aaronite priests from Aaron to Solomon, and although fourteen is a crucial number in the Temple blueprints for the perfect sanctuary, and although the rabbis may have named fourteen intermediaries in the transmission of the Torah down to Hillel and Shammai, the number fourteen is not prominent in Jewish tradition. Note that, in his *Gnomon*, Bengel attributes to a certain Rabbi Bechai the opinion that David was the fourteenth from Abraham on account of the value of David's name.

4. Joseph A. Fitzmyer, S.J., *The Gospel According to Luke* (Doubleday, 1979), vol. 1, p. 340.

5. Sermon on the Mount

AFTER THE BAPTISM of Jesus in Matthew's Gospel and the initial gathering of disciples, the first and longest of the work's five discourses occurs, explaining what is to be expected of Jesus' followers. This has normally been called the Sermon on the Mount—Augustine wrote a book under that title—though it is more a compendium or handbook of Christian ethics. Matthew puts together—from Mark, the Source (Q), and his own traditions—what became in effect the "the greatest hits" of New Testament sayings. Matthew chapters 5–7 are the most quoted part of the Christian Bible, containing not only the Beatitudes and the Lord's Prayer and the Golden Rule, but sayings about the light of the world, the salt of the earth, the lilies of the field, the tree known by its fruit, and the house built on rock instead of sand (among other familiar things). Some would be content if everything else in the New Testament had perished but these three chapters remained. They think it contains the essence not only of Matthew's Gospel but of Jesus' entire teaching.

After John the Baptist has heralded the arrival of the Mes-

SERMON ON THE MOUNT

siah, Matthew shows Jesus instituting the Messianic era. For that purpose, he describes Jesus as ascending a mountain—like Moses going up Sinai—to legislate a new order. What this entails is made clearest in the so-called Antitheses (5.21–48), but Jesus does not begin with those programmatic statements. He opens the sayings with a list of comforting felicitations (called *makarismoi*, from the word for "happy" used in the Beatitudes, *makarios*).

The Beatitudes (5.3–10)

MOSES' REVELATION came as a series of prohibitions ("Thou shalt not"). Jesus begins the Sermon on the Mount with messages of comfort, what was called in antiquity a *consolatio*, an address to those afflicted, neglected, or persecuted.

> "Happy the poor in their own mind,
>   since heaven's reign belongs to them.
> Happy the sad,
>   since they shall be consoled.
> Happy those who yield,
>   since they shall acquire the earth.
> Happy those who hunger and thirst to see right prevail,
>   since they will eat and drink their full.
> Happy those taking pity on others,
>   since they will be pitied.
> Happy those who are pure within,
>   since they will see God.

Happy those who bring peace to others,
 since they will be named God's sons.
Happy those who are punished for their virtue,
 since heaven's reign belongs to them." (5.3–10)

These are all paradoxes. They turn expectation and normal values upside down. The same paradoxical revaluing of all values (to use Nietzsche's term) is sounded throughout the Gospels—the last will be first, the slave will be master, those throwing away their life will save it, the suffering Messiah will win glory. But here there is a *concentration* of the ethical topsy-turvydom of Jesus' Revelation. To take the paradoxes one at a time . . .

1. *Happy the poor in their own mind.* Literally, the Greek says "the poor in spirit." But what does that mean? Clearly not the "spiritually impoverished" or those poor "in the Spirit." Those interpretations would not be paradoxes but flat-out contradictions. Jesus is saying that the mere physical condition of poverty is not the blessed state. He refers, rather, to those who accept poverty in their own mind as a state that does not make them envious of the rich or rebellious against providence. They have escaped the condemnation of the rich that Jesus pronounces when he says that they have their reward. Even those who are not physically poor can have the attitude of poverty that Jesus is blessing here—they stand poor in the sight of God, without the arrogance or oppressiveness of the rich. To stand with the poor is what Jesus calls for, as when he says (in this Gospel) that those who enter the reign

78

of heaven are those who fed the hungry, clothed the naked, and welcomed the foreigner (25.31–46). They enter heaven's reign, as this first Beatitude promises.

2. *Happy the sad.* The ultimate paradox is here—happy the unhappy! Again, it is not mere physical affliction or loss that Jesus is describing, but a spiritual state, a grieving for spiritual reasons. Augustine said that grieving over material losses is a sin: "The only lamentable thing is lamenting their loss, or rather not to lament lamenting them" (*Confessions* 10.1). Those sad for the right reasons are engaged in a virtuous act, and the assurance of that will in time be their comfort.

3. *Happy those who yield.* The "yielding" people in this statement are often translated as the "meek," the "mild," the "gentle." But that might just refer to those *unable* to be assertive. Jesus praises those who could be aggressive but who refuse to be. The full force of the paradox comes from the reward of yielding, since acquisition of the world is normally the prize of conquest. Jesus forswears conquest. The only lasting possession is not the one seized but the one given away.

4. *Happy those who hunger and thirst to see right prevail.* The contrast between physical condition and spiritual intention is again made clear. The appetite for the right is not the same as the body's need for sustenance, but it is aptly compared with it. The prevalence of the right is not a luxury item but an absolute need, as absolute as the body's need for what fuels it.

5. *Happy those taking pity on others.* One's own needs should not be directly addressed. By entering into the plight of others, one finds a response that covers one's own plight.

6. *Happy those who are pure within.* Literally, "the pure in heart." This is contrasted with the Jewish Holiness Code that made one unclean according to external things one dealt with. Jesus constantly broke through the taboos of the Holiness Code, embracing every kind of unclean person—Samaritan, leper, prostitute, menstruating woman, tax collector. Matthew later quotes Jesus as saying, "What a man takes into his mouth does not make him unclean. What comes out of his mouth—that is what can make him unclean" (15.11). It is this internal purity that the Beatitude felicitates. It looks straight at God, not at all the external ceremonies set up to hedge him off from the profane.

7. *Happy those who bring peace to others.* This again sets the right priority. By looking to the plight of others, restoring their good relations, one acts as God's emissary and earns the right to be called God's son.

8. *Happy those who are punished for their virtue.* Persecution, accepted for the right reasons, is a cleansing act. It cauterizes. It is a baptism "with fire."

The last Beatitude and the first one form "bookends," since they promise the same reward—possession of the reign of heaven. This proves that the eighth Beatitude is the final one. But some take the statement that follows as a ninth Beatitude. It is true that it begins with the same adjective, "happy" (*makarioi*). But this is an expansion of and commentary on the eight blessings. Its different function is signaled by the fact that it shifts from the third to the second person, saying, "Happy are *you* when . . . ," and continues with advice on how to conduct themselves in the state being felicitated.

> "Happy are you when they revile you and punish you and make every charge against you because of me. Be of good cheer and joyful, since your recompense is plentiful in heaven. For that is how they punished the prophets before you."
> (5.11–12)

The Antitheses (5.21–48)

THE BEATITUDES are a kind of overture to the whole long Sermon. The statement of the main theme is the new Law that Jesus enunciates, not replacing the old Law but fulfilling it (5.17–19), going beyond it, laying an obligation more internal than ceremonial. His followers must be *more* observant even than the strictest Pharisees (5.5), but with a different kind of observance, what Paul called "a circumcision of the heart" (Romans 2.29). Jesus' new legislation is pronounced in six commandments.

The six new commandments are called the Antitheses because they take the form *"You have heard . . . but I tell*

you. "[1] The new obligations are not relayed from God through
Moses. Jesus issues them on his own immediate authority (*"I
tell you"*).

1. Here is the first one:

"You have heard the directive to those of the old order, 'You
shall not murder—the murderer will be subject to trial.'
  "But I tell you that anyone who is angry with his brother
will be subject to trial. But anyone who calls his brother
'idiot!' will be subject to the Sanhedrin [court]. But anyone
who calls his brother 'subhuman!' will be subject to Gehenna's fire."

The hyperbole of this passage is the obverse side of the command to love in this Gospel. If love is the supreme and all-
encompassing obligation, then departures from it swiftly
escalate into desertion of that standard. Jesus expands this
concept by saying that one cannot pray to God if one has
offended another—one must leave the altar at once and make
recompense for the wrong. Love for fellow human beings is
the prerequisite for any profession of love for God. The old
order was handed down from on high, from Sinai, and it
looked first to God, to submission to him. The new order
works from the bottom up, since Jesus is now down among
those he loves and teaches us to love.

2. The next antithesis deals with inner purity, the subject
already of the sixth Beatitude, now fleshed out in detail.

"You have heard the directive, 'You shall not commit adultery.'

"But I tell you that anyone who looks at a woman with desire for her has already committed adultery inwardly. If your right eye makes you fall, rip it out and cast it away, because it is better for you to lose one part of your body than for all of it to be cast into Gehenna. And if your right hand makes you fall, chop it off and cast it away, because it is better for you to lose one part of your body than for all of it to be cast into Gehenna."

Purity was a matter of ceremonial usage in the old system. Jesus is not fulfilling that with a cancelation but with a stricter code, entirely internal. Purity is a matter of *intention.*

3. The third antithesis also introduces a stricter rule.

"It was also directed, 'Whoever dismisses a wife must give her a separation document.'

"But I tell you that anyone dismissing a wife, except for unchastity, makes her commit adultery, and if he marries a dismissed woman, he is an adulterer."

Matthew repeats this directive later (19.9). A patriarchal society demands virtue of wives as the only guarantee of the legitimacy of offspring. If the wife is untrue she may present her husband with a child not his. Jesus restricts divorce to this sole exception.[2]

4. The fourth antithesis continues the emphasis on personalism, making truthfulness not a juridical concept but a matter of inner integrity.

"Once more, *you have heard* the directive to those of the old order, 'Be no oath breaker, but honor oaths to the Lord.'

"*But I tell you,* swear no oaths at all—not by heaven (since it is God's throne), and not by earth (since it is his footstool), neither on Jerusalem (since it is the Great King's city), nor by your own head (since you cannot change a single hair of it to black or white). Let your word for 'yes' be 'yes,' for 'no' be 'no.' Going beyond that is for the Evil One."

Why should oath taking be treated as prompted by the Evil One? Because oaths were so frequently used in magic.[3] To swear by the stars was to invoke their power. That is why Jesus says that these are the dwelling places of the one God, to be disposed of only by him, not invoked for the swearer's own purpose.

5. The fifth antithesis transcends the *lex talionis*.

"*You have heard* the directive, '[Compensate] an eye with an eye, a tooth with a tooth.'

"*But I tell you,* oppose not one wronging you. Rather, when one punches your right cheek, offer him the other. To one suing for your shirt, give your coat as well. And if a man commandeers your services for a mile, provide it for two miles. Give to whoever asks, and turn not away requests for a loan."

As a teacher of nonviolence, Jesus goes beyond Tolstoy, Gandhi, Thoreau, and Dr. King.

6. The final antithesis takes us to a deeper level than the preceding one. There it was said that one should not use violence upon another. Here it is said that the restraint should be based on love.

"*You have heard* the directive 'You will love those near you and will hate those opposed to you.'

"*But I tell you*, you will love those opposed to you, and pray for those who persecute you, in order to be sons of your Father in heaven, who makes the sun rise over bad and good, and sends rain upon those in the right and those in the wrong."

Jesus is initiating the reign of heaven, when God's viewpoint will be everything. The prayer that he now teaches his followers is a prayer that this reign be confirmed.

The Lord's Prayer

IN ACCORD WITH the emphasis on religion as an inward activity, Jesus now warns against being public in one's charity, prayer, and fasting (6.1–18). On prayer he says this:

"When you pray, be not like the pretenders, who prefer to pray in the synagogues and in public squares, in the sight of others. In truth I tell you, that is all the profit they will have. But you, when you pray, go into your inner room and, locking your door, pray there to your Father, who is in hiding, and he, seeing you in hiding, will heed you. But when you pray, do not babble on as the pagans do, who think to win a hearing by the number of their words. So be not like them, since your Father knows what you require before you ask him." (6.5–8)

Then Jesus gives them the kind of prayer they should use. It is called his own prayer by long usage. It is not a prayer that has obvious Christian terms, and some have called it a Jewish prayer adopted for some reason by Matthew.[4]

But the Greek words for "your design be fulfilled" are exactly those Matthew describes Jesus as using in the garden of Gethsemane (26.42). The word for "design" is literally "what you will," but the agonizing choice of Jesus shows that he sees the overall plan of salvation depending on his submission to it, and the Christian prayer should reflect this acknowledgment of the great design of God. Furthermore, the petition "bring us not to the Breaking Point" reflects what Jesus also says in the garden: "Pray that you do not reach the Breaking Point" (26.41). The Breaking Point, both in history and in the individual encounter with history, is the *Peirasmos*, the great Test of all history. These clauses show that this is an eschatological prayer, and the final clause in it refers not to delivery from evil *(poneron)* but from the Evil One *(Poneros)*.[5] Jesus in the garden is saying that his encounter with the powers of darkness on this night is the pre-enactment of the final struggle that will end history with the triumph of the Father.

These parallels show that the Lord's Prayer is an eschatologically Christian prayer, with one sentence of three petitions directed at the vindication of God in the final showdown of history and a second sentence of three petitions asking that those who pray may be protected through this ordeal.[6]

> "Our Father of the heavens,
>   your title be honored,
> your reign arrive,
>   your design be fulfilled
> on earth as in heaven.

> "Our meal still to come
>   grant us today,
> and clear our moral account with you,
>   as we clear our account with others,
> and bring us not to the Breaking Point,
>   but wrest us from the Evil One."

"Our meal still to come" translates *artos epiousios*, where the rare adjective is derived either from *ep(i)-ienai* ("to come") or *ep(i)-einai* ("to be"). The King James Version took the latter sense, and translated "our daily bread" ("our being-now bread"). But the eschatological setting of the whole prayer shows that this is a reference to the coming meal of the heavenly completion. This End Time banquet is what Jesus refers to in this Gospel when he says, at the Last Supper, "I tell you that never again shall I drink this product of the vine until I drink it with you, a new wine, in my Father's reign" (26.29). The Lord's Prayer asks for an anticipation of this great feast. The prayer for the dismissal of debts ("clear our account") refers to the great Jubilee when all debts were canceled. This, too, is eschatological.

The whole prayer is pervaded by the action of God. The first three petitions are in the "passive divine imperative"— one cannot order God to fulfill his will. God's transcendent glory is celebrated. The emphasis is on *your . . . your . . . your.* The next three petitions express human needs, with repeated *our . . . us . . . our . . . our . . . us . . . us.* Only God's action can alleviate our peril.

Setting Priorities

THE REST OF the Sermon on the Mount (6.19–7.27) uses various teaching devices to set priorities in the light of the eschatological vision of the Lord's Prayer. Jesus tells his followers to lay up spiritual treasure where no moth or rust can consume it; to keep the heart pure and the eye single; to serve a single master, not two masters; to leave how one lives to the Father; to refrain from judging others; to give to all; to seek with trust; to beware false prophets; to build on a solid foun-

dation. The message throughout is one of reliance on the
Father:

"Do not trouble your mind about living, how you will eat or
drink, or about your body, what you will wear. Is not your
living more than what you eat, and your body more than
what it wears? Observe the birds in the sky—they do not
plant, or harvest, or store in barns, yet your Father in heaven
nourishes them. Are you not more precious than they? Who
of you can by worrying add a measure to his height?

"And why trouble yourself about what you will wear?
Take a lesson from the lilies in the field, how they blossom.
They do not toil, nor do they spin. Yet I tell you that not even
Solomon in all his dazzle was clothed as any one of them.
And if God clothes this way the plants in the field, which last
today and tomorrow are thrown in the fire, how much more
you, little as you trust him?

"So do not trouble yourself, asking, 'What will we eat?' or,
'What will we drink?' or, 'What will we wear?' All this is what
unbelievers worry about. Your Father in heaven understands
all your needs. But seek you first God's reign, and your right
standing with him, and all the rest will be supplied you. So do
not be troubled about tomorrow. Tomorrow will be troubled
over itself. Today's troubles are enough for today." (6.25–34)

Jesus uses several times the a fortiori argument ("If this . . .
then *how much more* that?"). If God clothes lilies so, then
how much more will he clothe you? If you give your children

bread instead of stone, then how much more will the Father give you (7.11)? In the case of the lilies, an extra strength is added to the punch line by the intermediary introduction of Solomon in all his splendor. Chesterton analyzed the passage brilliantly:

> There is perhaps nothing so perfect in all language or litera-
> ture as the use of these three degrees in the parable of the
> lilies of the field; in which he seems first to take one small
> flower in his hand and note its simplicity and even its impo-
> tence; then suddenly expands it in flamboyant colors into all
> the palaces and pavilions full of a great name in national leg-
> end and national glory; and then, by yet a third overturn,
> shrivels it to nothing once more with a gesture as if flinging
> it away: "and if God so clothes the grass that today is and
> tomorrow is cast into the oven, how much more . . ." It is like
> the building of a good Babel tower by white magic in a
> moment and in the movement of a hand, a tower heaved sud-
> denly up to heaven on top of which can be seen afar off,
> higher than we had fancied possible, the figure of a man; lifted
> by three infinities above all other things, on a starry ladder
> of light, logic and swift imagination.[7]

This part of the Sermon is full of glittering aphorisms, injunctions, and pithy statements, which stick in the memory. They are part of Matthew's teaching aim in this Gospel, though their heavy derivation from Q probably means that they reflect the original style of Jesus' teaching. The most famous and important of these brief directives has been referred to since the Middle Ages as the Golden Rule: "Whatever you would have people do for you, do that for them— such is the Law and the prophets" (7.12). This is another summary of the Antitheses, where it is said that love for others, even for one's enemies, is the Law and the prophets. The powerful leverage of this single sentence has often been demonstrated. One of my favorite examples of this is the use Quakers made of it in eighteenth-century Philadelphia. At a time when slavery was accepted all through the United States—when even men like Jonathan Edwards and Benjamin Franklin and Benjamin Rush owned slaves, because both the Jewish and the Christian Scriptures did not forbid slavery— men like Anthony Benezet and Jonathan Woolman said that all other scriptural defenses of the institution were abrogated by the Golden Rule. Do you wish others to make a slave of you? No? Then you must not make slaves of them.

Other memorable sayings in the Sermon include these:

> "Where your treasures are stored, there as well will your
> heart be." (6.21)
> "You cannot be the slave of God and of Greed." (6.24)
> "How is it you see a dust speck in your fellow's eye and
> cannot feel the block of wood in your own eye?" (7.3)
> "Do not throw your pearls down to pigs." (7.6)

The Sermon ends with the words "And it happened that, after Jesus had completed this speech . . ." (7.28). A similar or identical conclusion marks the end of each of the succeeding discourses (11.1, 13.53, 19.1, 26.1).

The five discourses are spaced almost evenly throughout the run of the Gospel, and each has a predominating theme. Matthew strives for an encyclopedic collection of the sayings of Jesus, and he spreads them out for maximum impact. After the longest discourse, the Sermon on the Mount (5.3–7.27), the *second discourse* (10.5–42) issues instructions for proselytizing others, forming a kind of missionary code. The *third discourse* (13.2–52) is a collection of the teaching parables, with rules for their interpretation. The *fourth discourse* (18.1–35) tells the followers how to conduct themselves toward one another, with mutual deference. The *fifth discourse* (24.4–25.46) is second only to the Sermon on the Mount in length. It describes the End Time, telling the followers how to face its troubles and reassuring them that the Lord will triumph. This completes the Matthean *Summa Theologiae*.

NOTES

1. The Antitheses resemble the classical trope called in German a *Priamel*—a statement of some value or values commonly held, with a counterstatement expressing a personal value.

2. Roman Catholic canon lawyers tried to close the exception by translating "except" as "not even for," but that forcing of the language has been abandoned, as Hans Dieter Betz notes: *The Sermon on the Mount* (Fortress Press, 1995), pp. 849–50.

3. Ibid., p. 271.

4. The most notorious claim that the prayer is not Christian comes from the postmillennial Christians' favorite scriptural commentary, *The Scofield Study Bible*, ad loc.

5. Since the genitive of both words is the same, the meaning is established

here by context, and by parallel uses, like Matthew 13.19, "the sons of the Evil One" *(Ponerou).*

6. The neat symmetry of the two sets of three petitions must be the result of Matthew's orderly arrangement of his material, as opposed to the shorter form Luke reports (Lk 11.2–4), apparently drawing on Q.

7. G. K. Chesterton, *The Everlasting Man* (Dodd, Mead & Company, 1947), pp. 244–45.

6. Death and Resurrection

THE CORE OF belief in Jesus (the Kerygma) is the climax of each Gospel, the long account of Jesus' death and the Resurrection. This was the basic message Paul had received: "that Messiah died for our sins, in accord with the Sacred Writings; and that he was buried; and that he rose on the third day, in accord with the Sacred Writings" (1 Corinthians 15.3–4). The same basic truth is enshrined in the early creeds, in the second clause of both the Apostles' Creed and the Nicene Creed. The accounts of the Passion are basically the same in each Gospel, which is what makes them orthodox and accepted as canonical. There are differences, of course, but most of them are minor. If certain details are omitted by this or that author, that does not mean that the author is ignorant of them. For instance, Matthew and Luke both knew and used Mark, but neither of them includes the names of Simon of Cyrene's sons or the detail of the man fleeing naked from the scene of Jesus' arrest. Those details meant nothing to their audience.

Similarly, only Matthew tells how Judas returned his blood money and hanged himself. This does not necessarily mean that the others did not know this—they may simply have felt that it was implicit in Jesus' condemning words.[1] Other differences reflect the different traditions available to each evangelist. The Synoptics speak of Jesus being tried before Jewish authorities in two stages, first in the high priest's quarters, then before the Sanhedrin. But John has him taken first to the father-in-law of the high priest, Annas, and omits any mention of the Sanhedrin. For a long time, this was taken as a proof that John, as the last Gospel in time, was farther from accurate information. But there is reason to think that John had the best sources for the Passion in general. This is confirmed by his dating of the events.

All three Synoptics say that Jesus was arrested, tried, and executed on the feast of Passover—which was begun at sundown of the preceding day and was followed by a week to celebrate the feast of Unleavened Bread. The Last Supper, the agony in the garden, the arrest in the garden, the hearing before Jewish authorities took place on the night before Pilate's trial and condemnation to execution. That all this was accomplished in the midst of celebration of the Passover is improbable, and it conflicts with what is said in the Gospels themselves—that the Jews wanted Jesus dispatched *before* the feast. The chief priests and scribes say in Mark (14.2), "It must not be done during the feast, lest it cause a popular uprising."

The sequence in John is more plausible, as are other aspects of his account. He has the Sanhedrin meet to plot Jesus' death well before Passover. Then Jesus goes to Bethany six days before the feast, and enters Jerusalem (greeted with palms) five days before the feast. His arrest and execution take place

on the night and day *before* Passover, and Jews taking him to
Pilate cannot enter the proconsul's quarters, "lest they be
made unclean with the Passover *at hand*" (18.28). They will
eat the Passover meal that night, *after* the death of Jesus. (4B
1356–76)

It is easy to see why the Synoptics would think Jesus died
on the Pasch. From earliest days Jesus was thought of as the
sacrificial (Paschal) lamb. Paul writes (1 Corinthians 5.7–8),
"Our Paschal lamb, Messiah, is sacrificed, so we should keep
the feast not with the old leaven, the leaven of wrongdoing
and evil, but with the unleavened bread of simplicity and
truth." When Jesus approaches John the Baptist, he is hailed
as "Lamb of God!" in John's Gospel (1.29)—so John thinks
of Jesus as the Paschal sacrifice, though he does not think he
was killed on the actual Pasch. There was no need for that
chronological confirmation, however naturally the other Gospels assumed such a fitting date.

"His Blood Is Ours"

THE EVANGELISTS, while adhering strictly to the Kerygma,
highlighted different events as they assumed new meaning
for the community each was addressing. We have already seen
that in the case of Mark addressing a people under persecution—the way, for instance, he draws a parallel between the
frightened women who find the empty tomb and the defect-
ing women of his own group. The actions of the Jews against
Jesus are also colored in different ways depending on the

relations with Jews experienced by the members of each community addressed by an evangelist. We saw that with Mark, where the Jewish Zealots had driven Jesus' followers into Syria. We can see it, too, in Matthew, where conflicts with the synagogues in Antioch seem to be at stake. In fact, Matthew seems to reflect the greatest degree of hostility between Jews and Christians. This goes against many assumptions that make John the most anti-Semitic Gospel. I believe the spectrum of hostility, moving from lowest to highest, runs from Luke to Mark to John to Matthew. Matthew, after all, has the verse that has had the most poisonous effect down through history: "His blood is ours, and our children's" (Mt 27.25).

That verse was unfortunately translated in the King James Version as "His blood *be* on us." This suggests that the respondents to Pilate outside his headquarters can take over God's determination of the fate of his chosen people. (That they remain his chosen people Paul asserts over and over in the Letter to the Romans.) This sentence contains one of those "marketplace Greek" shorthand forms that can be so misleading. There is no verb in it—the words are simply "His blood upon us." This "upon us" construction is a possessive and means "of us"—"ours." The bystanders say the blood belongs to them. It is presented in answer to Pilate's statement that he has no part in this bloodshed—though he alone can order it. What the bystanders say takes responsibility for the particular act; it is not a curse for all ages. It is meant as a persuasive prod to Pilate, who would like to kill Jesus without admitting that he is killing him. The bystanders give him an out, saying the act will be theirs, not his.

This worst of Matthew's words about the Jews is not quite as bad as Christian anti-Semites would make it in future years, but it is bad enough, reflecting the bitterness between Jews and Christians in Antioch. But Matthew does not let Pilate and the Roman authorities escape the blame for Jesus' death. Pilate alone has authority to execute criminals—another point on which John's Gospel is more accurately explicit than the others (4B 338, 363–72).

Pilate's Wife

ACCORDING TO MATTHEW, Pilate had the opportunity of better guidance from his wife, whose dream makes her send a message to Pilate: "Nothing to you and to this upright one" (Mt 27.19)—another of those marketplace Greek sayings without a verb, here meant to warn her husband against an action God disapproves of. I mentioned earlier, when treating Matthew's birth narrative, how that account was meant to be a bookend to the Passion narrative. There were divine-revelation dreams in the birth narrative, not only those given Joseph, but a dream given to Gentiles, to the Magi. That dream is here balanced against another dream for a Gentile, Pilate's wife. The Magis' dream directs them away from the guilty action of Herod, who wants to kill Jesus (like Pharaoh scheming against Moses). Pilate's wife tries to forestall the guilty action of her husband. But he ignores her dream—or rather, perverts it by saying he has nothing to do with the killing of this man, *while he kills him* (27.25).

Matthew perfectly catches the psychology of a person who denies that he is committing a sin in order to commit the sin. He uses a very strong verb, *apenipsato* (27.24): "He scrubbed one hand against the other." I translate the word as scrubbed, not merely washed, since it has a strong prefix, *ap-* ("off"). And I add "one hand against the other" since Greek has an extra grammatical "voice" that we lack in English. We have an active voice for verbs of doing something and a passive voice for verbs of being acted upon, but the Greeks had a middle voice for acting *upon oneself.* That is what is being described when Pilate scrubs *himself.*

After Pilate turns Jesus over to his Roman soldiers, they scourge him. This was part of the sentence of crucifixion. The prisoner was subjected to the lash to break his spirit and prevent resistance at the scene of execution. But the soldiers improvise their own further torture in a mock coronation scene. They give him a royal robe, a scepter, and a crown (27.28–29). Then they prostrate themselves before him in feigned reverence. Matthew, like Mark, calls the crown "of thorns" *(akanthōn).* Crowns at the time were wreaths or diadems. A wreath of thorns seems an unlikely part of this hastily improvised scene—thorns did not grow around Jerusalem, and wreathing them would be difficult. Brown follows others in thinking that the crown was made of acanthus leaves (4B 866–67). The words for "thorn" *(akantha)* and "acanthus" *(akanthos)* have the same genitive plural *(akanthōn),* the form used by Matthew. The crown, like the scepter and robe, is an instrument of mockery, not of torture.

Simon of Cyrene

ALL THREE Synoptics say that Simon of Cyrene carried the cross of Jesus. As was noted earlier, this is probably an accurate historic detail, since Mark's community knows the sons of Simon. Later Christian art would show Simon assisting Jesus in carrying the cross. But the artists were thinking of the entire cross, the heavy upright as well as the crossbeam. But in fact a prisoner carried only the crossbeam, tied across his shoulders. The upright would already be planted and standing in the place of execution. There is no way Simon could assist if the crossbeam were tied over Jesus' shoulders. The evangelists simply say that Simon carried it—obviously it had to be strapped to *his* shoulders.

Why would Jesus be spared a normal part of the crucifying sentence? Why would a stranger be dragooned on the spot into this hard and humiliating task, for which he had committed no crime? The only plausible explanation is that the scourging had left Jesus too weak to carry his own cross. The idea of Jesus as a perfect athletic specimen is belied by Pilate's surprise, expressed in Mark's Gospel (15.44), that he died so soon on the cross, where long hours and even days of pain were part of the cruel ingenuity of this worst form of punishment. This relatively quick death may have something to do with the form of Jesus' punishment.

There were two ways to affix a person to the cross, by nails or by rope. We might suppose the former the more cruel method. But since the nails were driven through the wrist, not the palm of the hand (where the body's weight would tear through the interstices of the fingers, giving no fixed point), the possibility of a quick death, as by slashing one's wrists, was greater (4B 929–51). The long torture of hanging on the cross, with the wrenching pressure on the arms and the difficulty of breathing except by lifting oneself up by aching arms, was more assured by the use of rope. That Jesus' extremities were pierced we know from the risen Jesus' reference to his wounds, so he probably died soon (relatively) of the nail wounds.[2]

The End

ARRIVED AT the place of execution, Jesus was stripped naked and the executioners cast lots for his clothes. Then the mockery of Jesus as a phony king was continued. Pilate posted the inscription *King of the Jews* on the cross, and the chief priests and scribes called out, "He is the king of Israel. Let him come down off the cross and we will believe in him" (27.42).

Aside from a loud cry just at the point of death, Jesus says only one thing from the cross in Matthew's Gospel. This accords with the impression of physical weakness given by the need to draft Simon into the problem of getting Jesus to the cross. The one thing the weakened Jesus says is an expression of extreme isolation and desolation: "My God, my God, why have you abandoned me?" (27.46). Since both Mark and Matthew quote this cry in the Aramaized Hebrew, there is every reason to think these are Jesus' very words *(ipsissima verba)*. This is the first line from Psalm 22, which portrays the suffering of a just man. Jesus resorts to the Sacred Writings as his last resort of prayer. Every human agency has turned against or abandoned Jesus, and no divine rescue has come. Jesus even uses a title that he never invoked elsewhere in the Gospels—"my God." In all other places, even in the desperate straits at Gethsemane, he always speaks of and to "my Father" or "the Father."

> Mark [like Matthew] calls our attention to this contrast between the two prayers [in the garden and on the cross] and makes it more poignant by reporting the address in each prayer in Jesus' own tongue: "Abba" and "Eloi," thus giving the impression of words coming genuinely from Jesus' heart, as distinct from the rest of his words that have been preserved in a foreign language (Greek). As he faces the agony of death, the Markan Jesus is presented as resorting to his mother tongue. (4B 1046–47)

Though Jesus undergoes the ultimate fate of being human in a fallen world, his words are still a prayer, an address to the distant God, and one calling on the tradition of his people, with all its hope in the promise that God has stayed with them through their travails. Jesus has relived that suffering of his people, and he will vindicate the promise on which it all was based.

Raymond Brown argued that Matthew, in the birth narrative, drew upon folkloric material like the later mystery plays. Matthew does the same thing in the Passion narrative, adding details mentioned only by him—the dream of Pilate's wife, the washing of the hands, the hanging of Judas, the portents at Jesus' death, the centurion's profession of faith, the guards posted at Jesus' tomb. The portents have an eschatological symbolism, to show the breaking of history into two eras, that before and that after the death of Jesus:

> Jesus again shrieked with a mighty voice and yielded up his life. And see! the veil of the Temple was torn, top to bottom, into two parts, and the earth quaked and the rocks split open, and graves yawned and many bodies of the holy dead were raised and emerged from the tombs [after he was raised], and entered into the holy city and appeared to many people. But the centurion and others attending on Jesus saw the earthquake and the other phenomena and they were deeply panicked, saying, "Surely this was the son of God." (27.50–54)[3]

Matthew had presented the coming of the Messiah as a cosmic event, heralded by the star of Balaam's prophecy. Now he presents Jesus' death as a world-rending event, echoing apocalyptic passages like Ezekiel 37.12: "Oh my people, I will open your graves and bring you up from them." Matthew's picture resembles that of later painters who conflate the crucifixion with the Last Judgment, the saved (the holy women, the much-loved follower) on Jesus' right, the damned (Roman and Jewish officials) on his left. The painters were prompted in part by the story in Luke of a thief who will be taken to heaven, always placed pictorially on Jesus' right, and the blaspheming thief on his left. A dramatic presentation of Matthew's scene can be found in the large Cremona fresco of the crucifixion by Pordenone, where rocks crack open in front of the cross, and the hooves of a Roman soldier's horse slip and clatter as earth gives way under it.[4]

Guards at the Tomb

ANOTHER FOLKLORE motif that Matthew uses was clearly meant to counter a story that he reports, a claim by "Jews" that Christians stole the body of Jesus from his tomb and then fraudulently asserted that he had come back to life (28.11–15). The story of guards posted at the tomb was clearly a popular tale meant to discredit the discrediting story. That the tale pre-existed Matthew's Gospel is indicated by the fact that the Gospel of Peter, a second-century noncanonical text, uses the same basic story, but seems not to draw directly from Matthew but from Matthew's popular source (4B 1305–10). In Matthew, the chief priests and the Pharisees go to Pilate on the Sabbath morning and ask him to post soldiers for sealing the tomb and standing guard over it, lest the followers of Jesus steal his body. Why do the Jews themselves not do this? Sealing the tomb and standing guard would be a form of work on the Sabbath. Besides, they might want the independent testimony of Roman soldiers that the body was secured. Also, the Jews would not want any role in dealing with Jesus' corpse, since crucifixion made a man unclean (Deuteronomy 21.23).

Why would Pilate agree to take responsibility for guarding the corpse? (He, after all, had not wanted to be responsible for the execution.) The Jews could persuasively argue that if the body of Jesus were stolen, the tumult Pilate wanted to prevent would follow. There is nothing implausible in the story, and that other Gospels omit it could mean simply that the rumor of the body's theft was not used in their region. But Raymond Brown argues that the guard story fits ill with the story of the women's visit to the tomb, and concludes that the popular tale was created to assert the reality of the Resurrection—a reality affirmed in the other accounts, even without the guard.

In Matthew, when the women come to the tomb, there is an earthquake and an angel rolls away the stone covering the tomb's opening—to reveal that the tomb is empty.[5] The angel tells the women to go tell the followers that Jesus is risen, and these women, unlike the ones in Mark's ending, leave on that errand. Only then are the guards mentioned again. They presumably see the angel and the women, and go to the chief priests (not to Pilate), who bribe them to keep the story quiet. The joins between the two stories Matthew is dealing with show as clearly as did the joins between the two stories he combined in the birth narrative—the story of the Magi and the story of Herod's search for the child. Guards and women seem not to notice their simultaneous presence on the scene.

But Matthew does manage to form a symmetry between his opening and his closing sequences. In both, he alternates divine activity and resistance to that activity. In the birth narrative, the three dreams of Joseph (to accept Mary as his wife, to take mother and child to Egypt, and to return from Egypt) are interspersed with attempts by Herod to take the child's life. In the burial narrative, the actions of Jesus' followers are interspersed with efforts to baffle them. I print here the good actions in boldface and the bad ones in Italics:

BIRTH NARRATIVE	BURIAL NARRATIVE
Joseph's dream (1.18–25)	**Burial of Jesus (27.57–61)**
Magi with Herod (2.1–12)	*Guards requested (27.62–66)*
Joseph's dream (2.13–15)	**Empty tomb (28.1–10)**
Massacre of innocents (2.16–18)	*Guards bribed (28.11–15)*
Joseph's dream (2.19–23)	**Jesus appears (28.16–20)**

This outline follows Brown's discussion of the passages (4B 1302), and shows how carefully Matthew has made his opening and closing sections chime together.

Matthew, unlike Luke and John, describes no appearance of the risen Jesus to his male followers in Jerusalem. Jesus meets the women as they are speeding away from the tomb and instructs them to tell the men that he will meet them in Galilee, on a mountaintop, presumably the one where he delivered his Sermon on the Mount in this Gospel. When he appears to them there, some are at first not sure that it is he (28.17)—which fits the numinous aura of his risen appearances (see Mk 16.11–14, Lk 24.13–35, Jn 20.14, 21.4). It also accords with the tradition, treated earlier, by which the Lord "passes by" in the Sacred Writings and is glimpsed only indirectly. There is great psychological acuity in this matter-of-fact recording of mystery.

Matthew ends his Gospel with the Great Commission Jesus gives his followers on the mountaintop. Davies and Allison say this mandate "has been called the key to the gospel, and even something like a table of contents placed at the end."[6]

"Every kind of authority, in heaven and on earth, has been given into my hands. Therefore go out and teach all the nations, baptizing them in the name of the Father and the Son and the Holy Spirit, instructing them how to fulfill all I have enjoined upon you. And see! I am among you every day until the ending of the ages." (28.18–20)

This is the first explicit invocation of the Trinity in the Gospels, and it takes place in the citation of a baptismal formula as Matthew's community performed the rite. It is also rounds off a ministry that began with the baptisms of John. Matthew is the great teacher among the evangelists. It is not surprising that, over most of the ensuing Christian centuries, his has been the most influential Gospel, the one most used in Christian instruction, the one put first in the canonical collection.

NOTES

1. Though Luke says nothing of Judas's death in his Gospel, he does, in the Acts of the Apostles (1.18), say that Judas fell to his death.
2. The words of Jesus telling Thomas to put his finger in the wounds in his hands and side (Lk 20.27) offer no difficulty to the nailing through the wrist, since "hand" is an inclusive term, applying as well to the wrist as to the palm. The same is true of preachers' later use of Psalm 22.17, which says in the Septuagint (but not in the Hebrew), "They have dug holes in my hands and feet."

It is noticeable that the evangelists themselves, despite other use of this psalm in the Passion narrative, do not cite this verse.

3. The phrase "after he was raised" is not in Tatian's quotation of this passage in his *Diatesseron*. "It is likely a later gloss, presumably added to reserve to Jesus the honor of being the very first to rise from the dead"—W. D. Davies and Dale C. Allison, *Matthew: A Shorter Commentary* (T. & T. Clark International, 2004), p. 529.

4. Charles E. Cohen, *The Art of Giovanni Antonio da Pordenone: Between Dialect and Language* (Cambridge University Press, 1996), vol. 2, plate 232.

5. In Christian art, the stone is often shown being rolled away so that the body of Jesus can emerge (see, for instance, Tintoretto's *Resurrection* in the Scuola di San Rocco in Venice). But the Gospels never depict the Resurrection. The risen body did not need to have the stone removed, it could walk through physical obstacles, as in Jn 20.26. The seal on the tomb is put over an empty place.

6. Davies and Allison, op. cit., p. 545.

III. LUKE

Report from the Reconciling Body of Jesus

LUKE'S IS THE *longest Gospel (19,404 words), and it is only the first of a two-book set, followed by Luke's Acts of the Apostles, which is almost as long (18,374 words). The combined volumes of Luke (37,774 words) thus make up a quarter of the entire New Testament. They are longer than all thirteen of the letters attributed to Paul (32,303 words).*

Who was the man with this impressive output? It is generally conceded that he writes better Greek than anyone in the New Testament except the anonymous author of the late Epistle to the Hebrews. Jerome in the fourth century said, "Of all the Gospel writers, he is the most skilled (eruditissimus) *in the Greek tongue."[1] Luke uses a larger and more nuanced vocabulary than the other evangelists.[2] This led to early guesses that Luke was himself Greek, and writing for Greeks, which Raymond Brown considers likely.[3] Yet, even though Luke's Gospel begins with an elaborate prologue modeled on those of the classical and Hellenistic histories, it departs from those models by its disproportionate shortness and by the author's failure to identify himself in the opening sentence; and the rest of the Gospel does not sustain the artfulness of its beginning.*[4] *After an early section full of Hebraic canticles, Luke reverts to the add-on technique (parataxis) of his sources (Mark and Q).*

The title "Gospel of Luke," like the other Gospel titles, was not part of the original text, but was added in the second century. When people cast about for a plausible author named Luke, they seemed to find one in Paul's Letter to Philemon (1.24), which sends greetings from "Mark, Aristarchus, Demas, and Luke, my fellow workers." Luke's name occurs in two other letters not considered authentically Pauline. In 2 Timothy 4.11, Luke is said to be the only person still with Paul. In Colossians 4.14, "Paul" refers to "Luke the beloved physician." Relying on the latter passage, some have tried to find traces of medical vocabulary in the Gospel or Acts, but without success.[5] The idea that our Luke was a comrade of Paul also runs into serious difficulties, since Acts misrepresents Paul's deeds and whereabouts as we know them from the letters—which is not surprising when we consider that Luke never quotes, refers to, or betrays any knowledge of Paul's own letters (even the ones that supposedly refer to himself).[6]

Luke is often considered the most humane of the evangelists, since he alone tells such moving stories as that of the Good Samaritan, the Prodigal Son, and the Good Thief, and he shows special sensitivity to women, not only to the mother of Jesus but to the widow of Nain, to the woman who washes Jesus' feet, to the longtime cripple, the woman with a menstrual disorder, the woman with the lost coin, the woman with the small donation, the women who follow Jesus on his trav-

els in Galilee, as well as those he addresses on his way to Gol-
gotha. He is also called irenic, or ecumenical—a reconciler of
Jews with Romans, and even of Peter with Paul. This has
made him popular with those who want a less thunderous
Jesus. Dante called Luke "a describer of Christ's kindness,"
and Ernst Renan culled his Gospel "the most beautiful book
that ever was."[7]

Luke also has special liturgical interests. It has already
been mentioned that his account of the walk toward Emmaus
re-creates a Christian ceremony around the Sacred Writings,
the Eucharist, and a profession of faith. The hymns ("canti-
cles") of the opening of the Gospel seem to be drawn from
the singing of the early gatherings. This goes with the logis-
tics of Christian meetings in the Acts of Apostles, where the
reading of the "humane" parables would emphasize consola-
tion of the gathered Brothers and Sisters.

Since only Matthew and Luke give birth narratives for
Jesus, since they differ so, and since they show the Gospels'
way of using the Sacred Writings to explain the mystery of
Jesus, I spend extra time on Luke's birth narrative, as I did
on Matthew's.

NOTES

1. Jerome, First Letter to Damascus 20.4.4.

2. John C. Hawkins, *Horae Synopticae: Contributions to the Study of the Synoptic Problem*, 2nd ed. (Oxford University Press, 1909), pp. 15–23.

3. Raymond E. Brown, *An Introduction to the New Testament* (Doubleday, 1997), pp. 270–71.

4. Loveday Alexander, *The Preface to Luke's Gospel* (Cambridge University Press, 1993), pp. 26–30, 102–3.

5. Henry J. Cadbury, *The Style and Literary Method of Luke* (Cambridge University Press, 1920), pp. 39–54.

6. Luke makes Paul a student of Gamaliel, trained in Jerusalem, where he persecuted Christians, though Paul says, "I was not known by my features to the Judean gatherings in Messiah" (Galatians 1.22), and he did not go to Jerusalem until three years after he became a follower of Jesus (1.18). The "we" passages in Acts, where the author writes as if accompanying Paul, have been used to prove that he is the Luke of Philemon. But the "we" passages put the author in Palestine, and Luke shows an ignorance of Palestine, as well as of the letters that supposedly refer to him. The "we" passages do not of themselves indicate that only *one* companion is being included in the pronoun, and Luke could have been incorporating the record of another author or authors, as he incorporates hymns not written by himself. See Raymond Brown, *Introduction*, pp. 268–70.

7. Dante, *De Monarchia* 1.18, and Renan, *Les évangiles*, 3rd ed. (Culmann Lebvy, 1877), p. 283.

7. Nativity

ALTHOUGH LUKE'S first sentence promises to put in order traditions going back to "eyewitnesses" *(autoptai)*, his birth narrative can have no firsthand testimony, any more than Matthew's did. Matthew, as we have seen, drew on popular narratives dramatizing the Sacred Writings. Luke is even more liturgical—he relies on songs created by the early communities. The change from his polished first sentence to the Semitic patterns of the "canticles" raised questions in the past about Luke's ethnic and linguistic background—did he know Hebrew, to create such striking poems? The answer is probably that Luke, as he assures us, is drawing on the traditions of the communities he writes for, where the Christian poems he puts in the mouth of Mary and Simeon were performed.

Annunciation of the Baptist's Birth

AS WAS MENTIONED earlier, Luke is more interested in the priestly traditions of the Sacred Writings than in kingly ones. The first annunciation in his narrative is not to Joseph, a Davidid, as in Matthew, but to a priest as he officiates in the Temple, Zechariah, who is told that his barren wife will have a child, who will be called John. The providence of the Lord in keeping the Jews' line intact is often symbolized in the birth of children from apparently barren women—Rebekah (Genesis 25.21), Rachel (Genesis 29.31), Hannah (1 Samuel 1.2). But only one couple resembles Zechariah and Elizabeth, in that *both* husband and wife are beyond the child-begetting age. That other couple is Abraham and Sarah, who beget Isaac (Genesis 18.11). Luke's use of poetic speech is already present in the repetitive patterns of the angel's annunciation to Zechariah. This may be the best place to point out that the principal metrical unit for Hebrew poetry is the paired clause, a second (or third) line echoing, supplementing, or defining the first (sometimes by contrast). This kind of poetry fills the early passages of Luke. The angel tells the Baptist's father:

"Have confidence, Zechariah,
    for your plea has been granted,
and your wife, Elizabeth, will bear you a son,
    and you will give him the name John.
and yours will be joy and delight,
    and many will rejoice at his birth.

"For he will be great in the eyes of the Lord,
    and no wine or strong liquid will he drink,
and he will be filled with Holy Spirit,
    even from the womb.

And many of Israel's sons he will guide
   toward the Lord their God.
and he will go before his gaze
   in the spirit and might of Elijah
to turn the fathers' hearts to their children,
      and resisting peoples to the minds of the just,
      to make ready for the Lord a receptive people." (1.13–17)

Abstention from wine and strong drink marks John as a Nazirite, one dedicated to the Lord from birth, like Samson (who was also born to a barren woman; Judges 13.2–3, 5). This Nazirite will look forward, so he does not do what traditional Jews did—tell sons to learn from their fathers. In the new order, the angel says, fathers will learn from their sons.

Annunciation of Jesus' Birth

THE ANGEL who appeared to Zechariah is nameless, but the angel who comes to Mary is Gabriel, the traditional name of the angel who drove Adam and Eve from Eden (Enoch 27). The fall is being reversed for this new Eve. When the angel appeared, Mary "was stunned *(dietarachthē)* and trying to puzzle out *(dielogizeto)* what kind of greeting this was" (1.29). The angel reassured her:

"Have confidence, Mary,
   for you have been favored by God,

WHAT THE GOSPELS MEANT

and—see!—you will conceive in your womb
    and bring forth a child.
He shall be great,
    and be called Son of the Highest.
And the Lord God will give him the throne
    of David his father,
and he shall reign over Jacob's line
    for ages without end." (1.30–33)

Mary asks, "How can this be, since I have not lain with a man?" The angel answers,

"Holy is the Spirit coming over you,
    and the power of the Highest will cloud you in glory,[1]
so the child who will be born to you
    will be called the holy Son of God." (1.35)

She responds: "See me, here, the Lord's slave. Let it happen as you say."

    To prove that nothing is impossible with God, Gabriel tells Mary that her aged cousin Elizabeth has already conceived a son. Mary hurries to Elizabeth so the two mothers can ponder what miracles they are carrying. Mary's song to Elizabeth is that of the triumphant women of Jewish history. Here is Hannah at the birth of Samuel:

"My heart rejoices in the Lord,
    In the Lord I now hold my head high,

My mouth is full of derision of my foes,
Exultant because thou hast saved me." (I Samuel 2.1)

Here is Judith after vanquishing Holofernes:

"God, even our God, is with us,
to show his power yet in Jerusalem,
and his force against the enemy,
as he hath done this day." (Judith 13.11)

The hymn of Mary resembles such songs so closely that some have thought it not a Christian hymn at all, but a Jewish poem put to new use. Raymond Brown argues that it is a Jewish Christian hymn, probably used in the liturgy in connection with the coming of the Messiah. Luke puts the poem in Mary's mouth, making her the spokesperson for the whole community.

"My soul expands toward the Lord,
and my spirit is glad in the God who rescues me,
since he looked from on high to his servant's lowliness,
for—see!—from now on generations shall bless me,
for the Powerful has done wonders for me,
and holy is his title.

"And his mercy is from one generation to the next,
toward those who hold him in awe.
He has flexed his right arm's might,
he has swept the haughty off in their hearts' mad dreams,

he has brought down the lofty from their thrones,
    and lifted up the lowly.
He has filled the hungry with good things
    and sent the rich away destitute.

"He has gathered in his servant Israel,
    in memory of his mercies,
as he promised to our fathers,
    to Abraham and his offspring without end." (1.46–55)

Augustine reminds us that we cannot make God any greater than he is. We cannot "magnify" him. We can only make him a greater part of our own inner hope and love, expanding toward him.

Birth of the Baptist

To KEEP running his parallel between the Baptist and Jesus, Luke reverts to John and tells of his birth before describing that of Jesus. When Zechariah repeats the angel's instruction that John shall be his son's name, he sings his *Benedictus*, second only to Mary's *Magnificat* in the famous songs of this opening sequence in Luke:

"Blessed is the Lord God of Israel,
    since he has cared for his people
    and wrought their release.
And he raised the victory sign of our rescue
    in the line of David, his son,

as he spoke through the mouths of his holy ones
    the prophets down through the ages,
of rescue from our enemies,
    and from the hand of those hating us,
to work mercy for our fathers
    and remember his holy covenant,
the oath he swore to Abraham our father,
    to draw us, free of fear,
    safely from our enemy's hand,
to serve him in holiness and justice
    under his gaze for all our days.

"And you, child, will be called a prophet of the Highest,
    you will advance under the Lord's view
    to prepare his ways,
to bring his people to knowledge of their rescue
    with release from their sins
through the inmost workings of his mercy,
    as he oversees the rising from on high,
shining on those who sit in darkness and death's shadow
    directing their feet along the path of peace." (1.68–79)

Birth of Jesus

MATTHEW DESCRIBED Mary and Joseph as living in Bethlehem, since that is where the Davidid Messiah was supposed to be born. Luke has a better tradition, that the family lived in Nazareth. How, then, could he get them to Bethlehem for the birth? He says that Caesar Augustus ordered a worldwide census by which people had to be registered at their birth-place—and Joseph, as a descendant of David, had therefore to go to Bethlehem. No relatives were there to welcome him, and the only lodging was full, so Jesus had to be born in a stable, where he was laid in a hay trough ("manger"). The problem with this is that Augustus never ordered a worldwide census. Luke is confusing a nonexistent Augustan census with the famous and resented census in Judaea, that of Quirinius, that took place ten years after Augustus's death, and it did not cover Galilee.

Luke's reasons for connecting the Messiah's birth with Caesar and the census come from the situation of Jesus' people who *are* Jesus in his time. He is writing in the eighties or nineties, after the destruction of the Temple in 70. The Brothers and Sisters who fled Palestine during the later years of the Jewish War are deracinated from their Palestinian origins. Luke tries to re-establish the lineage of those early years, connecting believers back to Jerusalem and the Temple. He wants to assert that the believers in Jesus are not the same people who fought Rome, like the Zealots, or were punished by the crushing of the rebellion. In both his Gospel and the Acts he emphasizes the good relations his community has with Rome. A memory of Augustus calls up the reputation that emperor had as the establisher of world peace, a thing symbolized in the great Altar of Peace *(Ara Pacis)* that exists to this day in Rome.

On the other hand, the census of Quirinius was so resented that it helped ignite the Zealots' initial rebellion against Quirinius's Syrian prefecture. Joseph and Mary peacefully obey Augustus's decree, and they do not take part in the resistance to Quirinius's administration of it. They are as observant of Roman law as of Jewish rites. Luke will be insistent that Jesus is not of this world; but he is not a political rebel against it either. Luke's nativity scene has none of the bloody concomitants of Herod's slaughter in Matthew. The peaceful shepherds are alerted to the Messiah's arrival by angels—in this place where David had been a shepherd. The placing of Jesus in the hay trough reverses the hardness of heart that God laments in Isaiah 1.3, which says,

> The ox knows its owner,
>> and the ass its master's stall;
> but Israel, my own people,
>> has no knowledge, no discernment.

The baby is swaddled to recall how Solomon was wrapped in strait bands as a baby:

> I was nursed in swaddling cloths,
>> and that with care,
> for there is no king that had any
>> other beginning of birth. (Wisdom 7.4–5)

In the Temple as an Infant

As LUKE SHOWS Jesus observing the Roman law, so he emphasizes his obedience to the Jewish Law, under which he was circumcised on the prescribed eighth day of his life. Joseph and Mary, Zechariah and Elizabeth, and Simeon and Anna at the Temple are all just people under the Jewish Law. Luke wants to emphasize this even though he does not really understand the Law—he says that Joseph as well as Mary had to go to the Temple in Jerusalem to be purified after childbirth, which was not the case.[2] Only the woman was considered unclean after childbirth. When Jesus is brought forward for presentation in the Temple, Simeon, a devout and observant man, rejoices that the long wait for the Messiah is now ending:

> "Now, Ruler, you let me go
>   in peace, as you promised,
> since my eyes behold the rescue
>   you work out in view of all peoples,
> a light you unveil to the Gentiles
>   and a splendor to your people Israel." (2.29–32)

Then he predicts to the mother, Mary:

> "This very one—see!—is set for the fall or rise of many in
>   Israel,
>   to be a sign contested.
> And a sword will pierce your soul,
>   since the schemings of many will be laid bare.[3]" (2.34–35)

The prophetess Anna adds her testimony to the fulfillment of Israel's hopes, and tells many about the child (2.36–38). But the family of Jesus leaves the Temple and returns to a village obscurity.

Adolescent in the Temple

THE OTHER THREE Gospels say nothing of Jesus' upbringing. Luke makes one exception to this, to show how Jesus versed himself in the Law and the teachings of the Temple, and to signal the mysterious nature of his relations with others—in this case, with his parents. As often in the Gospels, one episode is recounted as a symbol of a whole *process*, of Jesus growing into his mission. Jesus is being prepared as prophets were in the Sacred Writings, marked out by God for prayer and study.

His parents went yearly to Jerusalem for the Passover feast. And when he was twelve years old, they went to the feast as usual, and when they had completed the feast days and were going back, Jesus stayed behind in Jerusalem, and his parents did not realize this. Thinking he was in the return party, they went on for a day before they began to look for him among their relatives and friends. When they did not find him, they went back to Jerusalem and searched for him. And it happened that they found him after three days in the Temple, seated among the scholars, both listening to them and asking them questions. All who heard him were astonished at his intelligence and responses. When his parents saw him, they were dumbfounded [*exeplagēsan*], and his mother said to

him, "How, son, could you do this to us? See! your father
and I have been searching for you in anguish *[odynōmenoi]*."
And he said to them, "Why did you search for me? Did you
not realize that I must be at my Father's?" They did not
understand what this saying signified. And he left with them
and returned to Nazareth and was obedient to them. And his
mother kept all he said for close scrutiny in her heart. And
Jesus grew up mentally and physically, favored both by God
and by men. (2.41–52)

That last sentence recalls the training of another prophet,
Samuel, who "as he grew up, commended himself to the Lord
and to men" (1 Samuel 2.26).

Luke's Genealogy

LUKE DOES NOT place the genealogy of Jesus at the beginning
of his Gospel, as Matthew does. There was a problem with
doing that in the Gospel as we have it, since it begins not with
Jesus but with the Baptist. He could not put the genealogy
of *Jesus* before the annunciation of *John's* birth. He might
have put the genealogy before the account of Jesus' birth, but
that would break the symmetry by which he pairs John's
annunciation-birth-naming with Jesus' annunciation-
birth-naming—unless he wanted to give a matching genealogy to John.

What seems the most natural place to put it is just before
the beginning of Jesus' public life—that is, just before his baptism by John. But it is delayed still further, and given only

after the baptism. That is because Matthew traces Jesus' line down from Abraham, while Luke traces it up to God himself. Since it has just been revealed, at the baptism, that "you are my son, my loved one, in whom I delight" (3.22), the genealogy, which follows immediately, is a gloss on those words, showing how Jesus derives his sonship from the Father, through that Father's people.

Luke's genealogy is, to a degree, more historically plausible than Matthew's—though historical plausibility is no more his concern than Matthew's. Luke has more names, though they still cannot fill in the long stretch of history being sketched—Luke gives us seventy-seven names, to forty-one in Matthew, and he adds a fourth time span (pre-Abraham) to Matthew's three. Moreover, he does not have Matthew's irregular descent through women, not to mention women of ambiguous reputation. Luke's aim, though, is the same as Matthew's—to situate the meaning of Jesus' messiahship in the context of Sacred History. He is able to do this through the early hymn traditions used to celebrate that messiahship. Once again, Raymond Brown has it exactly right when he says that the birth narratives meditate on the mystery of "the birth of the Messiah."

NOTES

1. The normal translation, "will overshadow you," suggests a darkening; but the same verb is used by Luke of the cloud of glory over Jesus at the Transfiguration (9.34), and it is used in the Septuagint of the cloud that fills the tabernacle with light at Exodus 40.35. This cloud is a nimbus or halo, much like the pillar of fire that leads the way through the desert.

2. Raymond Brown notes that if the medieval belief that Mary delivered Jesus without breaking her virgin hymen were true, she would not have needed purification (1B 437). The liturgical feast day of Mary's Purification used to be called Candlemas, which led Gilbert Chesterton to write a poem on the paradox of Mary's standing amidst "a thousand flames to purify the Pure."

3. For the translation of *dialogismoi* as "scheming," see 1B 441: "All fourteen uses of *dialogismos* in the New Testament are pejorative."

8. A Jesus for Outcasts

LUKE'S IS THE Gospel most interested in liturgical matters. We have seen how his story of the followers walking to Emmaus creates a symbolic version of the post-Resurrection Christian liturgy—meditation on the Sacred Writings, followed by a Eucharist and profession of faith in Jesus. That comes at the end of Luke's Gospel. At the beginning of the public ministry Luke gives us a pre-Resurrection liturgy in a synagogue. Jesus goes to the synagogue in his hometown, Nazareth, reads a prophecy of the Messiah's coming from Isaiah, and proclaims that he is fulfilling the prophecy. The angry community says he is a local figure with no right to such high pretensions, and the main body tries to murder him. This is not only a symbolic pre-enactment of his own death, but a demonstration of the way his followers would be cast out of the synagogues when they proclaimed their belief in him as Messiah.

Jesus responds with a forecast of his motion out toward the Nations (Gentiles) as a result of his rejection by his own. Two other prophets—Elijah and Elisha—are used to explain this action, and the whole of the Gospel from this point opens up the Jewish mission of the Messiah to non-Jews, and especially to Samaritans, using the two prophets as a warrant for this program. Jesus cites the case of Elijah from 1 Kings 17: After cursing the evil king Ahab with a drought on his land, Elijah goes to a Gentile woman in the Sidon area and asks for food and drink. When she gives him of her little, he blesses her with eschatological abundance, supplying her with bread and oil that do not decrease with consumption. Jesus says this is a type of the rescue that will reach the Nations after he is rejected "at home." Similarly with the other prophet: Elisha, in 2 Kings 5, cures the warrior Naaman of leprosy, though Naaman is not an Israelite. When Elisha will accept no reward, Naaman takes two mule loads of the sacred earth of Israel off with him, so he can worship on it, a type of the spread of the Gospel. This whole passage is a foreshadowing of what Luke's Gospel will say in its coming chapters:

And he went to Nazareth, where he had grown up, and entered the synagogue as was his custom every Sabbath, and he stood up to read, and a scroll of the prophet Isaiah was given him. And unrolling the scroll, he found the passage where this is written:

The Lord's Spirit is with me,
  since he has anointed me,
has sent me to bring the poor a revelation,
  to announce release for the imprisoned,
to give sight to the blind,
  to give to the oppressed release,
to proclaim the Lord's year of jubilee.[1]

And rolling up the scroll, handing it to the assistant, he sat down. And all the eyes of those in the synagogue were intent upon him. But he began to tell them that "this day the words of the Sacred Writings are fulfilled in your very hearing." And all admitted that he had said this, but were astounded that he claimed such favor for himself with his own lips, and they said: "Is this not simply Joseph's son?" And he said, "No doubt you will quote me the saying 'Heal yourself if you are a doctor'—what we hear you have done in Capernaum, do the like here in your own land." But he said, "In truth I tell you that no prophet is recognized in his own land. But I solemnly assure you that there were many widows in Israel in the time of Elijah, when there was a drought for three and a half years and a great famine occurred everywhere in the land, yet Elijah was not sent to any woman but the widow in Sarepta of the Sidonians. And there were many lepers in Israel at the time of the prophet Elisha, yet none of them was cleansed, only Naaman the Syrian." And all in the synagogue swelled with outrage when they heard this. And they cast him out of the town, and drove him to the brow of the cliff on which the city was built, in order to throw him over. But he melted from the crowd and departed. (4.16–30)

Since Luke is showing how Jesus will go out to the Gentiles, this passage is a symbolic forecast not only of his whole Gospel but of the succeeding book he will add to it, the Acts of the Apostles, which describes the spread of the Revelation to all nations. The economy and force of this episode are hard to overstate.

The Good Samaritan

THE ATTEMPT on the life of Jesus by his own townspeople is the equivalent of the murderous attitude of his brothers in Mark. Luke will contrast this attitude with the kindness of the despised Samaritans, a people unclean in the eyes of Jews at that time. The people of Samaria were geographically the "foreigners" nearest to Israel. They had their own version of the Torah and their own Temple. There was a historical hostility between the two peoples, such that Samaritans barred the way through their territory when Jesus' followers tried to pass through on their way to Jerusalem. The angry followers quote 2 Kings 1.10–14 where Elijah calls down fire from heaven against those who oppose him (Lk 9.54). But Jesus rebukes them, and they pass on. It is against this backdrop that Jesus tells the parable of the Good Samaritan. A lawyer has asked Jesus what he must do to achieve eternal life. When Jesus turns the question back on the questioner, asking him what the Law says, the man answers: "You will love the Lord God with all your heart and all your being and all your strength and all your intention, and love any near you as you do yourself" (10.27).

When Jesus approves this answer, the lawyer presses him further, asking who is near to one. Jesus, "seizing the opportunity" *(hypolabōn)*, responds:

"Once a man was going from Jerusalem to Jericho, and he encountered thieves, and they tore his clothes off and beat

him, and went away leaving him nearly a corpse. By chance
a priest was coming along on the same road, and seeing him
he circled far wide of him. In the same way, a Levite
approached the same spot and seeing him circled far wide of
him. But a Samaritan faring abroad came by and at sight of
him was deeply moved, and coming close he bandaged his
wounds, medicating them with emollients and astringents.[2]
And hoisting him onto his own beast, he led him to a public
lodging and committed him to its charge. In the morning he
took two denarii and gave them to the lodge host and said,
'Take charge of him, and any additional cost I shall cover on
my return.' Which of the three, then, treated the robbers'
victim as one near him?" "The one who took pity on
him." And Jesus told him: "From now on do the same."
(10.30–37)

This story is most often cited as an exhortation to univer-
sal kindness. But it also has a sting in it. The two who pass
the victim by are a priest and a member of the priestly family among the Jews, while the Samaritan is a non-Jew and an
unclean person by the priests' standard. The Holiness Code
forbids contamination from a corpse, and the victim is nearly
a corpse (hēmithanēs). So each of the pious men "circled far
wide of him" (anti-par-ēlthen). Once again, the Jews have
rejected what the Gentile favors. The same point is made when
Jesus cures ten lepers on the border of Samaria, only one of
whom is a Samaritan—and the Samaritan is the only one who
returns to give Jesus thanks (17.11–19).

The Woman with a Menstrual Disorder

JESUS HAS REGARD not only for Gentiles but for all outsiders—those neglected, despised, or outcast. The woman scorned by the Pharisees as a sinner is forgiven her sins because she has loved much (7.37–50). The humble tax collector in the back of the Temple is preferred over the proud Pharisee up front (18.10–14). The beggar Lazarus arrives at the reign of heaven while the rich Dives is excluded (16.19–31). Jesus' embrace of the despised is made very clear in the case of a woman with a perpetual menstrual discharge (8.43–48), a story Luke shares with the Gospel of Mark. Each month when a Jewish woman underwent her period, she had to go the Temple or to the ritual baths to be purified. So the woman with a perpetual discharge was permanently unpurifiable. She was not only barred from the Temple but all her dealings with others would make them unclean. She could not cook their meals or wash their clothes. According to Leviticus 15.25–27:

> When a woman has a prolonged discharge of blood at the time of her menstruation, or when her discharge continues beyond the period of menstruation, her impurity shall last all the time of her discharge; she shall be as unclean as during the period of her menstruation. Any bed on which she lies during the time of her discharge shall be like that which she used during menstruation, and everything on which she sits shall be as unclean as in her menstrual uncleanness. Every person who touches them shall be unclean; he shall

wash his clothes, bathe in water, and remain unclean until evening.

The woman in the Gospel story had been in this condition for twelve years, despite all her appeals for help to priests and physicians. But now, defying the ban on contact with others, she pushes through the crowd around Jesus and touches the tassels on his robe. He senses what has happened, and asks, "Who touched me?" (8.45). Peter tells him there is no telling, in such a jostle of people who could have touched him, but he says: "Someone touched me. I sensed power surging from me" (8.46). The woman in a panic confessed her effrontery, and said she had been instantly healed. Jesus said, "My daughter, it is your trust that has rescued you. Go on in peace" (8.48).

Sermon on the Plain

LIKE MATTHEW, Luke collects a number of sayings of Jesus into one long discourse. Many of Luke's sayings are variants of Matthew's, including a shortened form of the Beatitudes. But Matthew presents the sayings as delivered on a mountain and Luke describes them as spoken on "a level place" (6.17). Hence Luke's version is called the Sermon on the Plain by commentators, contrasting it with the Sermon on the Mount. Did Matthew expand Luke's thirty verses into his own 107 verses, or did Luke shrink the 107 down to thirty? The answer is that neither is reworking the other. Instead, each is using Mark, Q, and his own tradition to create his own summary of Jesus' teaching. Was the Sermon originally delivered on the

WHAT THE GOSPELS MEANT

mountain, or on a plain? Augustine cleverly argued that part
of the long discourse was given on the mountain to Jesus' close
followers, before Jesus came down to deliver the rest to a
larger audience.³ But the substance is the same in both versions, and the setting is clearly symbolic in both cases—Matthew using the mountain for an authoritative Sinai-like
delivery of the new Law, Luke choosing a lowly setting in
which Jesus could express and praise humility. Luke's Sermon,
though shorter than Matthew's, is also more rambling, without the didactic orderliness of the other evangelist.

Luke gives us four Beatitudes where Matthew writes eight,
and Luke puts them in the second person ("God's reign is
yours") where Matthew uses the third person ("God's reign
is theirs").

> "Happy the poor, since God's reign is yours.
> Happy the hungry, since you will be fed.
> Happy the weeping, since you will be laughing.
> Happy you whom men hate, and cast out and revile, and
> blacken your name for the Son of Man's sake. At such a
> time take heart and be frisky, for see! you will be many
> times repaid in heaven.⁴ For your ancestors treated the
> prophets that way." (6.20–23)

Luke fits to these four Beatitudes four antitheses, the so-called
Woes:

> "But alas for you rich, since you have used up your solace.
> Alas for you well-fed, since you will know hunger.

Alas for you who laugh, since you will grieve and weep.
Alas for you whom everyone flatters, since your fathers
    treated false prophets that way." (6.24–26)

In the rest of the so-called Sermon, Luke treats the same
themes that Matthew does—themes of loving enemies, of not
judging, of building on solid foundations—and does so with
his own kind of eloquence:

"I say to all you who can hear me: Love your foes, help those
who hate you, praise those who curse you, pray for those
who abuse you. To one who punches your cheek, offer the
other cheek. To one seizing your cloak, do not refuse your
tunic under it. Whoever asks, give to him. Whoever seizes,
do not resist. Exactly how you wish to be treated, in that way
treat others. For if you love those who love back, what mark
of virtue have you? Sinners themselves love those who
love back. If you treat well those treating you well, what mark
of virtue have you? That is how sinners act. If you lend only
where you calculate a return, what mark of virtue have
you? Sinners, too, lend to sinners, calculating an exact return.
No, rather love your foes, and treat them well, and lend
without any calculation of return. Your great repayment
will be that you are children of the Highest One, who also
favors ingrates and scoundrels. Be just as lenient as that
lenient Father. Do not judge, then, and you will not be judged.
Be no sentencer, and you will not be sentenced. Pardon
and you will be pardoned. Give, and ample recompense
of crammed-in, sifted-down, overtoppling good will be

showered into your lap. The excess will correspond to your
excess." (6.27–38)

One subject of Matthew's Sermon on the Mount Luke
deals with in a later passage, outside his own Sermon on the
Plain—the Lord's Prayer. Luke's "bare bones" version does
not have the neat symmetry of Matthew's two pairs of three
petitions. Some argue that this means Luke's version is the
more historically accurate report, drawing on an unadorned
Q Source. It is more likely that both versions reflect several
streams of tradition, none of them having the character of a
transcript. Here is Luke:

> "Father! your title be honored,
>   your reign arrive,
> our meal to come,
>   grant us this day,
> and dismiss our sins
>   since we have dismissed all our debtors,
> and bring us not to the Breaking Point." (11.2–4)

The Prodigal Son

PERHAPS THE most famous and loved part of Luke's Gospel is
the story known as the parable of the Prodigal Son.

> "There once was a man with two sons, and the younger of
> them said to his father: 'Father, give me my share of the
> inheritance.' So he divided up his livelihood. And not long

after, the younger son collected all his property and left his
homeland for a distant country, and there he wasted everything in wild living. After all his goods were gone, a harsh
famine hit the land. And he was beginning to starve. So he
picked himself up and went to work for a citizen of that country, who sent him onto his farm to tend pigs. And he eagerly
filled his stomach with the pods the pigs ate, since no one
would give him anything else. Then he reached the point of
saying to himself: How many of my father's workers eat well
while I am dying of hunger? I will get up and go to my father
and say, 'Father I have offended heaven in your full sight, I
no longer deserve to be called your son. Treat me as one of
your workers.' And he got up and went to his father. But
while he was still a long way off, his father saw him and his
heart melted, and he ran to grab him in a hug and kissed him.
But his son told him, 'Father, I have offended heaven in your
full sight, I no longer deserve to be called your son.' But his
father ordered his slaves, 'Hurry, bring out the choice rai-
ment and put it on him, and give him a ring for his finger
and shoes for his feet. Take the pampered calf and kill it, and
make a glad feast of it, since this son of mine was dead and
he lives, was lost and is found.' And they launched into the
feast." (15.11–24)

This first half of the Prodigal's story is tied back, with the
words "was lost and is found," to the two short parables that
precede this long one—the accounts of the one lost sheep and
of the woman's lost coin. Each of these tales ends with an
exclamation like that of the Prodigal's father. The shepherd

says, "Celebrate with me, since I have found the lost sheep" (15.6). The woman says, "Celebrate with me, since I have found the coin that was lost" (15.9). The moral of all these tales is given by Jesus himself: "I tell you accordingly that what cheers heaven is one sinner who reforms rather than ninety-nine virtuous who do not need reform" (15.7).

But is that fair to the virtuous, who never needed to reform? That problem is taken up in the second half of the Prodigal's story:

"But the older son was at work on the farm. And as he came back and approached the house, he heard music and dancing. And he called one of the slave boys to learn what was happening. And he told him that 'your brother is back, and your father has killed the pampered calf, since he got him back safe.' And he was angry and would not go in. And his father came out and was cajoling him. But in response he told his father: 'See all the years I have been slaving for you and never disobeyed your instructions, and you never gave me even a goat that I might have a feast with my friends. But when that son of yours, after wasting your livelihood on whores, comes back, you kill the pampered calf for him.' But he told him: 'My son, you are always by my side, and all I have is yours. But we must have a happy feast, since your brother was dead and he lives, was lost and is found.'" (15.25–32)

The two kinds of son recall the two groups sharing the favor of the Father throughout this Gospel—the Jews and the

Gentiles. But which is which? The richness of the parable comes from the fact that it can be read, as it were, backwards and forwards. Are the Jews good sons or erring sons? In one reading, the Jews will be the good son, who lives on the ancestral estate, an inheritor of the promise, by contrast with the Prodigal, who lives in a far (Gentile) country among strangers and unclean animals. But you can read it another way, that the Jews are the bad son, jealous of the admission of one who is now seen as an outsider. The bad son rejects the broader mercy of the Father. Which is the proper reading? I believe both are. It is an endlessly reversible tale of the Father's bounty extended omnidirectionally, to both kinds of son, the one who stays and the one who returns. Luke the irenic reconciler is at his very best in this parable that opens up endless mirrors of meaning.

Though it is probable that Luke never knew Paul, this parable shows that he agrees with Paul's attitude toward Gentiles and Jews. Paul believed that both peoples are called and both will be saved:

I would impress this secret providence on you, [Gentile] Brothers, to keep you from confidence in your own conceit—that part of Israel has lost its vision, but only until the full number of the Nations is brought in. Then all Israel will be rescued, as the Sacred Writings say: "Out of Zion comes the Rescuer, to rip away iniquities from Jacob, so my covenant abides with them, to remedy their sinfulness." They are now foes to the Revelation for your sake, but by their singling out they are the patriarchs' favored sons. God does not go back on what he gave them, they are his chosen ones. As you were outside the trust in God but are now spared, their betrayal of trust leads to your being spared—but they will be spared in their turn. God provides for the betrayal of all to bring about the sparing of all. (Romans 11.25–32)

That is, inadvertently, a way of telling the story of the older and younger brother in the Prodigal Son tale. I think it would be fair to describe the tale of the Prodigal Son as containing the inmost kernel of Luke's thinking and theology, according to which we are all outcasts, and Jesus is coming to rescue us all.

NOTES

1. The year of jubilee here is literally "the acceptable year" *(eniautos dektos)*, but the references to "release" show this is a jubilee year for canceling all debts. See Joel B. Green, *The Gospel of Luke* (Eerdmans, 1997), p. 212.

2. The emollients and astringents are literally "oil and wine," but medical versions of those items.

3. Augustine, *The Consistency of the Gospel Writers* 2.47.

4. "Be frisky" is, literally, "leap about" *(skirtan).*

9. A Healing Death

DESCRIBING JESUS' agony in Gethsemane, where he prays
that the cup of suffering be removed from him, Luke simpli-
fies the account given by the other two Synoptics. He does
this in order to add new material of his own—a common
Lukan practice in his Passion narrative (4B 183). Mark and
Matthew have Jesus return three times to find his chosen followers asleep. Luke has him return to them only once. He
wants to throw into prominence the words that he adds after
his prayer that the cup be taken away: "But an angel from
heaven appeared to him, giving him strength. And struggling
as he was, he kept praying more earnestly, and his sweat fell
in separate drops to the ground as if it were blood" (22.43–44).
Some editors of Luke's text delete these lines. The words are
absent from some ancient manuscripts, and they are put in
Matthew's Gospel by others.[1]

Brown concludes that the lines were more probably
removed from the original than added to it. Some later Christian copyist might have wanted to avoid the idea that an angel
would be stronger than Jesus—though angels minister to
Jesus after the trial in the desert (Mt 4.11). Others might have

doubted that a person can sweat blood. Yet the text does not say that the sweat *was* blood, but that it fell down as if *(hōsei)* it were blood—that is, in separate drops *(thromboi)*. Brown notes that the word for Jesus' struggle *(agōnia)* is used for athletic contests, where the contender is an "agonist" *(agōnistēs)*. The struggle with Satan that took place in the desert is renewed here:

> [G. G.] Gamba compares the strengthening role of the angel to that of a trainer who readies the athlete; the prayer of Jesus is the last-minute preparation. Unlike the disciples who sleep, Jesus is now poised at the starting line. (4B 189)

Jesus' Arrest

THOSE WHO THOUGHT of Luke as a physician noticed that he alone of the evangelists has Jesus heal the ear struck off in the struggle around his arrest. All four Gospels refer to this. Mark says that the ear was cut by a bystander (not, presumably, one of Jesus' followers, since he does not rebuke him in this Gospel). Matthew and Luke say an unnamed disciple resisted Jesus' arrest (though they display cowardice everywhere else in the Passion narrative). Only John says that it was Peter who wielded the sword—Peter, who is about to deny his master over and over. In Luke, Jesus tells the resister on his side, "Let them [his arresters] carry on" (22.51).[2] Jesus had earlier tried to brace his followers for the great trial coming upon them by saying they should buy a sword (22.36). That he meant this metaphorically is shown by his answer when they say their group has two swords among them. "Enough of this," Jesus remarks sadly (22.38). He has told them often enough not to be violent. In John's Gospel he will tell Pilate that his reign is not of this order—if it were, his followers would have fought for him (Jn 18.36).

Pilate and Herod

ALL THE EVANGELISTS present Pilate as a conflicted man not quite knowing what to do with Jesus. Would this mysterious Jew cause more trouble to the settled order if he lived, or if he were put to death? Pilate tries for a time to avoid settling that point. He offers to execute a different criminal, hoping that will satisfy the crowd's blood lust. To Pilate's puzzlement, the crowd says it wants to see Jesus die instead. Only Luke presents a special dodge Pilate uses to deflect responsibility from himself. Pilate is the prefect only of Judaea.[3] Rule over Galilee to the north belongs to the tetrarch there, Herod Antipas. Since most of Jesus' ministry took place in Galilee, and Pilate knew that the tetrarch was in Jerusalem during Passover, he tossed the hot potato over to Herod, with whom Pilate had been on uneasy terms in the past.

Herod Antipas, the successor-son of Herod the Great (who dealt with the Magi in Matthew), was glad to see Jesus. After killing John the Baptist, this Herod had been troubled by Jesus' apparent continuation of John's rabble-rousing. He wanted to learn more about Jesus, to test him, perhaps to kill him. In Luke, there is a long-distance mental fencing match between Herod and Jesus.

Herod the tetrarch heard all that was going on, and did not
know what to make of what was being reported—by some,
that John had come back from the dead; by others, that Elijah
had arrived; by others, that some ancient prophet had arisen.
But Herod said, "I decapitated John. Who is this man I
am hearing about?" And he desired to lay eyes upon him.
(9.7–9)

When Jesus began to move out of Galilee toward Jerusalem, some Pharisees warned or threatened him that he was
not escaping Herod's vigilance. They say:

"Take off from this place and go away, since Herod is seeking to kill you." And he says to them, "Go away and tell that
fox that, see! this day and the next I cast out devils and cure
the sick, and on the third day I reach my goal. But for this
day and the next I must fare on my way, since it is not des-
tined for a prophet to perish outside Jerusalem." (13.31–33)

So when Pilate sends Jesus over to Herod, Herod is happy
to see the man he was angling for delivered into his hands:

Pilate, after this report, inquired whether the man before him
was from Galilee, and learning that he was from that juris-
diction, he committed him to Herod, who was in Jerusalem
at the time. But Herod was extremely pleased to see Jesus,
since he had long desired to set eyes on him, because of what
he had heard of him. And he hoped to see some prodigy

wrought by him. But he probed him with many questions. But he made no answer at all. But the high priests and the scribes stood around perpetually questioning him. But Herod, along with his soldiers, after insulting and ridiculing him, and clothing him in a splendid robe, sent him back to Pilate. But Herod and Pilate became each other's friend on this very day, though they had been foes up to this point. (23.6–12)

We might wonder why Herod did not kill Jesus now that he had the chance. But it was clearly more diplomatic to let Pilate act within his own Judaean realm. Brown suggests that what Pilate wanted from Herod was an investigation *(anakrisis)* that would endorse Pilate's judgment, giving expert opinion from Jesus' first sphere of activity. The tetrarch's soldiers put a splendid *(lampra)* robe on Jesus in order to mock him as a king—and that would be the charge posted on the cross: "King of the Jews." The two rulers have bolstered each other's authority, forming a pact in the blood of Jesus. There can be no doubt who was guilty of Jesus' death. It was the two self-congratulating rulers, now made friends after long enmity.

The Way to Golgotha

IN LUKE'S GOSPEL, with its emphasis on women, women have traveled with him in Galilee (8.1–3), and they follow him to Jerusalem, where they watch the crucifixion from a distance (23.49) and go to tend his body in the tomb (23.55). But when Jesus is on his way to his death, he meets another group of women, Jewish sympathizers—"daughters of Jerusalem," not Galileans. Luke thus brings onto the scene of Jesus' death some Jews who are not hostile or derisive.

> A crowd of ordinary people came along, including women who beat their breasts and expressed their sorrow for him. But Jesus turned aside to them and said: "Daughters of Jerusalem, shed no tears for me, but shed tears for yourselves and your children, since, see! the time is at hand when people will say, 'Happy the childless, the wombs that bore none, the breasts that nursed none.' Then they will launch a cry to the mountains, 'Fall on us,' and to the hills, 'Hide us over.' Since if they do this to wood still green, what will happen to the dry?" (23.27–31)

The Jesus of Luke's Gospel thinks of others throughout his own ordeal. Here he is telling them of the fall of Jerusalem that will come upon them, and he echoes the prophet Hosea (10.8): "They will say to the mountains, 'Cover us,' and to the hills, 'Fall on us.'" When he says that the coming fury is such that green wood, not ready for burning, is heaped on before the cured wood, he is echoing Ezekiel 20.47, "The fire will consume all the wood, green and dry alike."

Death on the Cross

MARK AND MATTHEW record only one saying of Jesus on the cross, his cry of abandonment. But Luke and John each quote three sayings by him, with no duplication between them.

Luke's words are reconciling, in accord with his consistent picture of Jesus. Looking at all those responsible for his death, he prays: "Spare them, Father, since they do not understand what they are doing" (23.34). Those who want to affix blame for Jesus' death, and punish those who did it, go against the prayer of Jesus himself. That this was Luke's reading of Jesus' mind is clear from his Acts of the Apostles (3.17), where Peter tells the Jews: "And now, brothers, I realize that you acted without knowledge, as did your rulers. But this is how God accomplished the Messiah's death, foretold through the words of all the prophets." The tragic thing about later history is not simply that some Christians forget or defy Jesus' words, but that certain copyists may actually have removed them from the Gospel, not wanting to accept that Jesus would impose forgiveness for such a heinous act. The verse is missing from some manuscripts, and its removal is more likely than a later interpolation of it (4B 979–80).

The second saying of Jesus in Luke is also one of forgiveness and concern for others.

> But one of the criminals suspended there was taunting him: "Are you not the Messiah? Save yourself—and us." But the other responded, rebuking him: "Have you no fear of God? You are under the same sentence as he is; justly in our case, since we are getting what our crimes deserve, while this man broke no law." And he said to Jesus, "Keep me in mind when you enter your reign." And he said to him, "In truth I tell you: This day, with me, you will enter Paradise." (23.39 43)

This is the last chance Jesus has to break through the boundaries sealing off the "unclean," for this crucified man is, like him, under a curse according to the Holiness Code (Deuteronomy 21.22–23). But inner purity and trust take the criminal from his gibbet straight to heaven.

Luke's last saying of Jesus from the cross is a loud cry, "Father, I hand over my life into your hands" (23.46). The cross is an instrument of healing in Luke's vision of it. The Roman centurion who sees him die gives praise to God and says, "This man was without doubt one in the right" (23.47). And people went away beating their breasts in sympathy, as the daughters of Jerusalem had done before the execution (23.48).

The Risen Lord

A DISTINGUISHING MARK of Luke's Gospel is the way he treats Galilee as superseded by Jerusalem in the risen life of Jesus. That should surprise us. He, more than other any Gospel writer, dwelt on the importance not only of men but of women from Galilee. He knows them as a group and as individuals—Mary Magdalene, and Joanna, the wife of Chusa, Herod's steward, and Susanna, "and many others" (8.2–3). He knows they were there at the crucifixion. He knows that the Magdalene and Joanna, and also Mary the mother of Jacob, went to the tomb on Sunday morning (24.10). Yet these Galilean women are not told that Jesus will meet the men in their company in Galilee, as the women are told in Mark and Matthew. The whole risen experience in Luke takes place in

Jerusalem. That is where the activity of the Jesus movement will be launched in Luke's next book, the Acts of the Apostles, since Pentecost, the sending of the Spirit, occurs in the capital city.

For Luke, the reconciler, Jerusalem is a key symbol. The Gospel began with that city in the Temple scenes of the nativity story, and the Jesus story ends with Jerusalem in the Ascension and Pentecost accounts. This is important because Jerusalem had been destroyed at least a decade before Luke wrote and more likely two decades earlier. The whole action of the Jesus movement thenceforth goes forward—as it began with Paul—in the Diaspora, where more Jews lived than had remained in Palestine. All the New Testament texts are written in the Diaspora, and probably none was written in a more distant place than Luke's (Greece). There is a kind of compensatory yearning back to origins in Luke's fascination, almost obsession, with Jerusalem. He does not want followers of Jesus to be deracinated from their Judaean roots. He says that Paul was trained in Jerusalem and returned there more often than his own letters can verify. Luke is sympathetic to Jacob the brother of the Lord in his attempt to retain the Law and attend the Temple, so long as that is possible. Luke has hopes for observant Jews to come to a recognition of Jesus as the Messiah, the same hopes Paul had. After all, Luke's whole narrative of the Messiah's birth is centered on his reception by observant Jews—Zachary and Elizabeth and Simeon and Anna and Joseph and Mary.

I have already mentioned the way that the colloquy on the way to Emmaus re-creates liturgical scenes in Luke's time.

That same is true of the reaction when the two followers return from Emmaus and recount their experience to the other followers in Jerusalem. As they were speaking, Jesus appeared in their midst and gave the Last Discourse and Great Commission of Luke's Gospel.

> While they [the Emmaus pair] were telling their story, he stood among them himself. And he said to them, "Peace to you." Disoriented by terror, they thought they were seeing a ghost. And he said to them, "Why are you dismayed? And why do doubts disturb your spirit? Look at my hands and feet—it is I myself. Touch and look—no ghost has flesh and bones such as you see in me." And as he said this he showed them his hands and feet. But they were still doubtful in their joy, and wondering at it. He said, "Do you have something to eat?" But they offered him some fried fish. And taking this, he ate it as they watched. (24.36–43)

Paul, who had seen the risen Jesus, says that the risen body resembles the one that died as little as a seed resembles a full-grown plant; but there is some continuity between the spiritualized state and the past earthly life, a truth Jesus teaches in the most concrete way. John, too, has Jesus eat when he appears by the Sea of Galilee (Jn 21.13). Thus, in the words of the poet Denise Levertov, does Jesus

> give
> to humble friends the joy
> of giving Him food—fish and a honeycomb.[4]

At this point Jesus repeats the lessons he had given the two on the road to Emmaus, meditating on the Sacred Writings as all early Christians did in their liturgies:

> "These are the teachings I voiced when I was living with you, that all the Sacred Writings about me in the law of Moses and the prophets and the psalms had to be fulfilled." Then he opened their mind to understand the Sacred Writings. And he said to them that "in this way it was written that the Messiah must die and rise again on the third day, and a turn from sin be announced in his name to all nations. You, starting from Jerusalem, are to testify to these things. And see! I shed on you the revelation from my Father. But stay here in the city until you are clothed in power from above." (24.44–49)

Luke prepares here for the scene of Pentecost in the opening section of his second volume, the Acts of the Apostles, telling how the followers were indeed "clothed in power" by descent of the Holy Spirit, which made the previously timorous followers go out boldly and speak words that people from every nation could understand. Jesus the reconciler has sent people away from the cross—Jew and Gentile, daughters of Jerusalem and the centurion—to praise the Father in the new order inaugurated by his death and Resurrection.

NOTES

1. Brown argues that the words were joined to Matthew as part of a Holy Thursday liturgical reading, not as a textual judgment (4B 181).

2. Literally, the words say, "Allow even to this."

3. Pilate is often referred to as the procurator of Judaea, but that title post-dates his term. He was *praefectus* (4B 336–37).

4. Denise Levertov, "Ikon: The Harrowing of Hell," from *A Door in the Hive* (New Directions, 1989).

IV. JOHN

Report from the Mystical Body of Jesus

ONCE IT WAS *thought that the authors of John's Gospel and of the Epistles of John and the Revelation of John were one person, the apostle John, son of Zebedee, one of the Twelve, the Beloved Disciple referred to in the Gospel, the one who reclined on the breast of Jesus at the Last Supper and stood at the cross with Mary, the mother of Jesus. This is the figure who entered the iconography of Christian art, the John of many devotional pictures.*

There was always a problem with that view. To begin with, Revelation is written in ungrammatical Greek far removed from the style of the Gospel. Even more to the point, the Gospel itself does not seem to be written by one person, whether the son of Zebedee or not. It ends and begins again at certain points, it has repetitions that look like insertions by another hand. Two or three or even more are thought to have been involved in its production.

One of the older reasons for doubting that the Gospel was written by the Palestinian John is that its mystical (some say "Gnostic") theology was considered Hellenistic, perhaps Neo-Platonist, with its emphasis on the Word as Wisdom. That would help place the Gospel late enough to have emigrated out from its purely Jewish roots. And a late dating, along with its dissimilarity from the Synoptic Gospels, seemed to indicate that it was less historically reliable about the facts of Jesus' life and thought.

But it turns out that John is more accurate than the Synoptics on points of Palestinian geography, trips to Jerusalem, Jewish feasts, the chronology of the Passion, and other topics.[1] *Moreover, the Logos literature drawn on in the Gospel is that of Jewish Wisdom writings, not Platonic philosophy. This does not, of course, prove that the apostle was the evangelist. Raymond Brown originally accepted that hypothesis (2B lxxxviii–cii) but he later came to the view that the evangelist was a follower of "the Beloved Disciple," an unidentified intimate of Jesus who formed a community dedicated to the doctrines he learned from him (3B 189–98).*

Brown traced the development of this school, which produced at least three (and perhaps five) authors of the "Johannine" books—the Gospel, the Epistles of John, and Revelation. Brown describes the development of the Gospel itself as having three stages.[2] *First, the period when the Beloved Disciple followed Jesus, spread his words, and formed his school. Second, a time when followers of the Beloved Disciple taught and preached from the riches entrusted to them by the Beloved Disciple, culminating in the work of an especially talented follower, who wrote the first edition of the Gospel (this is the man Brown calls the evangelist). And third, the work of a redactor, who used some of the Beloved Disciple's teachings that the evangelist had left out. Though the redactor writes*

in the same literary style and mode of thought as the evan-
gelist, he was a different man. He does not revise the original
draft, but inserts his new material without making obvious
adjustments to the first text (3B 189–99).

According to this theory, John is still the latest of the Gos-
pels, written perhaps in the nineties and redacted at the begin-
ning of the second century (3B 213–15), but it draws on early
and sound traditions, carefully guarded by the school of the
Beloved Disciple, which seems to have been widespread
enough to have internal factions (reflected in the Epistles)
and to have been centered in Asia Minor, perhaps around
Ephesus.[3]

NOTES

1. For the accuracy of many traditions in John, see 2B xlii, lxxxii, xcviii, 850, 3B 200–02, 4B 1356–73, 1479.

2. Brown first thought that the Gospel was formed in five stages (2B xxiv–xxxix), but he saw later that the same process could be more compendiously described in three stages (3B 62–69).

3. See 2B cii–iii, 3B 204–6.

10. Word into World

AMONG THE FOUR evangelists John is sometimes called the Theologian, largely because of the high Christology of his opening hymn. When I was growing up in the 1940s and 1950s, the Catholic Mass regularly ended with a reading of that hymn, which gave an exalted and mystical air to our exit from the ceremony. Of the four animal symbols given to the evangelists, John's seemed the most appropriate—he was the eagle. Augustine put it this way:

> Of the four evangelists (or rather of the four books of the one Gospel), the holy apostle John—appropriately compared to an eagle because of his spiritual insight—gave his teaching a higher and far more ethereal arc than did the other three, and by this loftiness he wished our hearts to soar. For the other three evangelists were walking as it were along the ground with their human Lord, and they said little of his divinity. But this one, as scorning to walk along the ground, at the outset launched himself, with a lightning flash, not only up above the ground but above the encompassing air

and heaven, and above the ranks of angels and the whole range of invisible powers, and he rose through all these things to the One who made them—who told him, "At the origin the Word was, and the Word faced God, and the Word was God. He at the origin faced God. Through him all things existed, and without him nothing that exits existed." Everything else he taught in accord with this exalted opening, and he spoke as no one else has of the Lord's divine status. He breathed forth what he had drunk in.[1]

The claim that the whole Gospel accords with the opening is only partly true. Certain elements in the hymn are not repeated—Jesus, for instance, is never called the Word in the body of the work, and key terms in the hymn have no special later emphasis—"favor" *(charis)*, for instance, and "supremacy" *(plēroma)*.[2] That is one reason modern scholars think that the hymn pre-existed the Gospel, like the hymns Paul quotes at Philippians 2.6–11 and Galatians 3.26–28, or the canticles of Mary, Zechariah, and Simeon in the first chapters of the Gospel of Luke, or the hymn material used in the Letter to the Hebrews. Those show that the high Christology once called an invention of John (or Paul) actually existed in the earliest prayers of the Christian assemblies.

The Opening Hymn

THE SEPARATE EXISTENCE of the hymn in the first chapter of John's Gospel is indicated in several ways. For one thing, its

poetic structure is broken into by prose insertions that con-
nect the hymn with what immediately follows, an account of
John the Baptist (2B 21–23). This suggests that the Gospel
originally opened, as does Mark, with Jesus' meeting with the
Baptist (Matthew and Luke start their account of the public
life at the same point). The evangelist John, or his redactor,
was using a hymn from the Johannine community, but probably as an afterthought to the formation of the original text.
In that case, a hymn spelling out the Messianic meaning of
what follows has the same function as the birth narratives in
Matthew and Luke—only John goes back beyond the birth of
Jesus, and even beyond the creation of the world, to show God
in communion with the Word that will become flesh. Here is
the hymn without the prose insertions (whose places are
marked here as *w, x, y,* and *z*). I italicize the "staircase" words
that link verse to verse.

At the origin was the *Word,*
    and the *Word* faced God,[3]
and the Word was *God;*
    this faced *God* at the origin.

Through him all things came to *exist,*
    and without him nothing that *exists* existed.
What existed in him was *vivifying,*[4]
    and the *vivification* was a light to men,
and the light shone into the *darkness,*
    and the *darkness* did not cope with it.[5]
    [*w*]

He was in the *universe*,
 and through him the *universe* existed
 yet the *universe* did not recognize him.
He came to his *chosen* ones,
 yet his *chosen* did not welcome him.
But to all those who did welcome him
 he gave the privilege of being God's offspring.
 [*x*]
And the Word became human flesh
 and bivouacked with us.[6]
And we have seen his *splendor*,
 a *splendor* of God's only Son,
 supreme in favor and fidelity.[7]
 [*y*]
since of his supremacy
 we all have our share,
 favor answering favor.
 [*z*]

The prose insertions have two functions. Two of them—
[*w*] and [*y*] above—distinguish the Word of the hymn from
the coming of the Baptist, which follows immediately on the
hymn. The first insert warns that the coming of John is different from the coming of the light into the world, and adds
the further qualifier that John is not the darkness, or unable
to "cope with" the light:

A man was sent from God whose name was John, who came
for testimony, to testify to the light, so that all might believe

through him. He was not himself the light, but only came to testify to the light. The genuine light, which enlightens all men, was still coming into the universe. (1.6–9).

This is a kind of footnote to the hymn text, one incorporated into the text since papyrus scrolls admitted no footnotes.

A second reference to John the Baptist occurs at the place marked [y] above, and it footnotes the idea of the Word revealing its own splendor. John, it is said, simply foretold the splendor, without himself revealing it.

John testified to him and cried out as he spoke: "Here is the one I told you of. He comes behind me but is ahead of me, since he was before me." (1.15)

This anticipates what the Baptist will shortly be saying in the first episode of this Gospel (1.29, 35–36), and makes clear the double time scheme by which the Baptist precedes Jesus on earth but the Word precedes the Baptist in heaven. The words clearly assert the pre-existence of Jesus, and this footnote may be meant to emphasize that such is the proper understanding of the hymn.

Two other prose insertions clarify what the hymn has just said. As a footnote to the line about becoming God's offspring, John distinguishes the Word as God's Son from the derivative sonship bestowed on receivers of the light. The [y] insert thus reads:

. . . for those who trust in his title, who are not born of blood-line nor from flesh's desire nor from human design, but from God. (1.12)

A final clarification, the one marked [z] above, follows on the phrase "favor answering favor," showing that the favor (charis) coming from the Word itself is higher than that relayed through Moses. Moses spoke with God but did not see him. The Word has seen God.

—since, while the Law was given to Moses, favor and fidel-ity comes through Jesus Messiah. No one has ever seen God. God the only Son, in the very heart of the Father, is the one who reveals him. (1.17–18)

This is another clear assertion that Jesus is God. Either the evangelist or the redactor re-emphasizes that this is the under-lying premise of the hymn.

John the Baptist

THE FOUR prose insertions ease us into the story of John, who has twice been referred to in the course of the hymn's expo-sition. In paintings and statues of John the Baptist, he is often shown with a scroll containing the words, "Look! God's lamb!" These are usually presented in Latin, Ecce agnus Dei. The words do not figure in the three earlier accounts of the Baptist—only in John's, where the Baptist uses them,

emphatically, two times (1.29, 35). John is the one who introduces the note of a *suffering* Messiah from the very outset,
based on Isaiah's description of the suffering servant of the
Lord as a lamb.

> He was led like a sheep to the slaughter,
>> like a lamb that is dumb before the shearers.
>>> (Isaiah 53.7)

The reference is clear from the way the Baptist continues:
"Look! God's lamb, who will lift away the sins of the universe" (1.29), referring to the same song in Isaiah:

> But he was pierced for our transgressions,
>> tortured for our iniquities;
> the chastisement he bore is health for us
>> and by his scourging we are healed. (Isaiah 53.5)

The Baptist portrayed in John is far from the angry man
of Matthew (3.7,11). The latter denounces his auditors as
"snakes' offspring" and promises a cauterizing of their sins
("baptism by Spirit *and fire*"). Nor is John's the reforming
Baptist of Luke, telling soldiers to accept their wages (3.14).
John's Baptist says that Jesus will baptize only with Spirit, not
with fire. More to the point, *he never baptizes Jesus.*

In the Synoptics, Jesus is publicly proclaimed the Son of
God as he comes out of the water of baptism. In John, the
Baptist has a private revelation. The other three have the voice

of God calling Jesus his Son only after he is baptized. Here, John alone sees the Spirit descending on Jesus as soon as he catches sight of him. I give the passage of John, italicizing the redactor's addition to it:

> The next day he sees Jesus coming toward him and says: "Look! God's lamb, who lifts away the sins of the universe! Here is the one I told you of. He comes behind me but is ahead of me, since he was before me. I did not recognize him myself, but that he would be revealed to Israel is the very reason I came to baptize with water." And John also gave testimony in these words: "I saw the Spirit coming down as it were a dove from the sky, and it hovered over him. *For I did not recognize him, but the one who sent me to baptize with water told me: 'The one on whom you see the Spirit descend and hover, that is the one who is to baptize with the Holy Spirit.' I saw him myself, and have given my testimony, 'This man is marked out by God.'* " (1.29–34)

The last verses are a perfect example of the redactor's work, who adds new material without changing the original text, a sign of his respect for it. The other examples of this redactor's work are so obvious that there is no need to keep pointing them out, except for special purposes.

Since in this Gospel there is no public manifestation of Jesus' status at the Jordan, it is only the Baptist's testimony that guides Jesus' first followers to him (Jn 1.35–37). The public manifestation of Jesus' power first takes place in John through a miracle that only this Gospel reports—which indicates that the Beloved Disciple was present at the miracle and passed it on as important to his school.

The Miracle at Cana

JESUS BRINGS HIS first followers to a wedding, where his mother tells him that the party has run out of wine. He answers: "What to me and to you, woman? My time is not yet come" (2.4). Then he quietly changes the water in huge stone vessels used for purification into the finest wine—six vats in all, each holding fifteen to twenty-five gallons (2.6). That means he supplied the party with between ninety and 150 gallons of wine, far more than any party could drink—and that is the point. This is a sign of the Messianic age's surplus, described in the Sacred Writings as a superabundance of delightful things—a land flowing with milk and honey (Exodus 3.8), a river flowing with honey (Job 20.17), bread showered from heaven (Exodus 16.4), trees bearing fruit every month (Ezekiel 47.12), an overflowing cup (Psalm 23.5), what the Gospel of Luke calls "ample recompense of crammed-in, sifted-down, overtoppling good" (Lk 6.38). Why did Jesus perform this miracle though he said his time had not yet come? A Mariolatrous answer in the past was that he broke the Father's redemptive schedule to please his mother, despite his abrupt dismissal of her words—a deep misunderstanding of his relation to the Father. Jesus' time is set by the Father, and is not his to break. Nor does John show any special esteem for the mother of Jesus (who is not even named by him)—Luke is the only evangelist who praises her.

Though Jesus says his time is not yet come, he gives a sign of what that time will mean when it does come—that he will be revealed in his Passion and Resurrection as initiating the Messianic age. That is the intention of the sign, and it has the desired effect on his disciples, for whom this is the first hint of his divinity. "He showed them his splendor, and the followers believed in him" (2.11).

The Cleansing of the Temple

JOHN, LIKE THE Synoptics, recounts how Jesus drove the money changers out of the Temple precinct. But the other three put the event at the very end of his public ministry, just before his arrest, and they make it the cause of his death. John's dating of it could not be further from theirs—he puts it at the very outset of Jesus' ministry. There are two reasons for this. Only he includes the raising of Lazarus in his Gospel, and he makes that the cause of Jesus' death. So Raymond Brown and others say that Lazarus displaced the Temple event. But that does not explain why John moved it so far back from the Passion narrative.[8] To see that we must consider another reason for the story's placement.

John puts it first to present a background theme for all that follows. Matthew and Luke had done something similar when they prefaced Jesus' public ministry with his temptations in the desert. Those events were summary statements of a process—not only the process of Jesus' coming to grips with his identity and mission but the process that will be played out over and over as he moves toward his death, a struggle with the reign of evil in the world. Jesus' whole life is a contest with the demonic. That is the struggle that is signaled, as by a musical prelude, in the multifaceted encounter with Satan in the desert.

In the same way, Jesus' rejection of Temple sacrifice is a statement of the meaning that will be played out over and over in John's Gospel, where he rejects the ceremonial and external observances of religion to stress that religion is an inward matter of the heart, of the direct encounter with the Father through Jesus himself. He will tell Nicodemus that the inner rebirth is a matter of love, not law. He will tell the Samaritan woman that worship will no longer be in her Temple at Gerizim or in the Jews' Temple in Jerusalem—and that cleanness will not come from the proper handling of the water she gives him but from a fountain springing up within. He will contrast the Bread of Life with the "clean" foods of the Holiness Code. He will tell the adulteress that her life is not forfeit to the external law if she has a saving love. He will finally engage the Temple authorities in the contest that leads to his Passion.

For all these encounters the issue is first stated when he drives out the money changers in the Temple. Those scholars who say he has not the stature at the outset of his ministry to make such a dramatic and climactic move are missing the point: he is implicitly overturning the Temple in all he does during his public life. The cleansing of the Temple is the statement of a theme. Jesus is completing the mission that many prophets had taken on in the criticism of religious externals. Jesus says that the money changers are making his Father's house "a traders' mart." Zechariah had said that in the Messianic time "no trader shall again be seen in the house of the Lord of Hosts" (14.21). Malachi had said that the Lord would come to the priests in the Temple and "he will purify the Levites and cleanse them like gold and silver" (3.3). Jeremiah had quoted the Lord: "Do you think that this house, this house that bears my name, is a robbers' cave?" (7.11). Jesus, by his actions, says that the Messianic day is come.

Only John says that Jesus twined cords into a little scourge with which to threaten the money changers, enacting the Father's anger. His followers recalled the Sacred Writing, "Zeal for your house will devour me" (Jn 2.17)—Psalm 69.9 in the Septuagint says, "Zeal for your house has devoured me." The shock of bystanders is understandable:

> The Jews spoke out at this and said: "What authorization can you show us that you do this?" Jesus answered and told them: "Bring down this Temple, and in three days I shall raise it up." To which the Jews answered: "This Temple was built over forty-six years, and you will raise it up in three days?" But he was speaking of his body as the Temple. After he was resurrected from the dead, his followers recalled how he had said this, and they came to believe in the Sacred Writings and in the word he had spoken. (2.18–22)

The community of the Beloved Disciple, as it reflected on the meaning of this emblematic prelude to their own writings, would realize that they were the Temple that Jesus had raised, as members of his mystical body. As Paul had said, "Do you not recognize that you are God's Temple, and the habitation of God's Spirit is in you?" (1 Corinthians 3.16). It is the message of the inner life that this community will especially ponder and treasure—as we see in the events John is about to report.

NOTES

1. Augustine, *Interpreting John's Gospel* 36.1.

2. See 2B xxiv, 19. Though Jesus' discourses in this Gospel have a Hebraic repetitiveness, they do not have the tight interlocking progression of the opening hymn, with "staircase" technique (2B 19).

3. Literally, "the Word was *toward* [the preposition *pros*] God." Brown translates, "The Word was in God's presence." The point is that there is an interaction, a facing toward each other of the Word and God.

4. Brown argues that "the word for 'life' (*zoē*) never means natural life in John or the Johannine epistles. The identification of this life with the light of men in the next line makes us think that eternal life is meant" (2B 7). So I translate it as the life-*giving* (vivifying) life.

5. The verb I translate as "cope with," *katalambanein*, is literally "to take over." It can mean to subdue, or to make one's own (by, for instance, knowing), or to manage. I take it in the last sense, but the line is difficult, and that seems to be why the evangelist adds a prose note [*w*] to the poem he is quoting.

6. Literally "cast his tent with us," as God traveled with the tents of his people during the Exodus.

7. Literally "full [a superlative] of favor and truth keeping."

8. Brown opines that there might have been an early prediction of the Temple's fall, unaccompanied by the expulsion of the money changers, and when the time came to move the expulsion story back it was connected with the first mention of the Temple (2B 118).

11. The Inner Life

In the opening hymn of this Gospel it was said: "And the light shone into the darkness, and the darkness could not cope with it" (1.5). We are given a fulfillment of that statement in the story of Nicodemus, a prominent Pharisee—a member of the seventy-person ruling Sanhedrin—who comes to Jesus by night to ask him questions privately. He is impressed by Jesus, but plays it safe, apart from his fellows, and struggles in the dark to cope with the light that is coming into the world.

Nicodemus

NICODEMUS SUSPECTS that Jesus has come from God, but leaves that notion hanging in the air as he approaches Jesus clandestinely. Nicodemus asks if the meaning of Jesus' wondrous deeds is that God is with him. Jesus answers with words that show Nicodemus cannot "cope with" the light. He says that to see "the reign of heaven" one must undergo "a higher birth." The term Jesus uses for a *higher* birth is "be born *anōthen,*" where the adverb can mean "from above" or "again." John is returning to the point he appended to the opening hymn, saying that those reborn of God came "not from a human bloodline nor from flesh's longing, but from God"—a passage (we have seen) explaining the so-called virgin birth.

Nicodemus, not coping with the light, takes Jesus' saying in the earthly sense, as calling for a fleshly birth "again." He asks, "How can a man already old be born again? He cannot crawl back into his mother's womb and issue out" (3.4). Jesus answers what Nicodemus saw as a riddle with another cryptic saying:

> "In truth I tell you:
> Unless a man is reborn out of water and the Spirit,
>   he cannot enter into God's reign.
> What flesh produces is flesh,
>   what Spirit produces is spirit.
> Then do not be astounded at my word:
>   You must have a higher birth.
> The Spirit is a wind blowing where it will,
>   and what it is saying you hear,
> not knowing whence it issues,
>   or whither it passes.
> This is the state of one
>   who is brought forth of the Spirit." (3.5–8)

Nicodemus then asks how such a birth can occur. Jesus answers in a long discourse that "unpacks" what the opening hymn said about the Word facing the Father, coming into flesh, shining light in the darkness, leading to birth in the Spirit. What was given in an abstract way in the hymn is now made the personal message of Jesus at the outset of his ministry. This first long discourse spells out what Jesus will be *saying* in all the later events, as his cleansing of the Temple expressed what he will be *doing*. In that sense, it is a kind of bookend with the final discourse, given at the Last Supper, which expresses the meaning of Jesus as he will live on in his followers.

The Jesus of John uses a language different from that he used in the Synoptics. Though he does not speak in poems, strictly considered, he uses the Hebrew poetic patterns of repeated thoughts in pairs and triplets. This has made some scholars think that this Gospel has no relation to the historical Jesus—though many of the facts in the narrative sections are more accurate than parallel reports in the earlier Gospels. The Beloved Disciple has generally authentic traditions about what was done, though he does not pretend to be a stenographer of what was said. The Johannine school meditated on the fullest and deepest meanings of what Jesus said, and expressed those meanings more fully and at more length than if they were just reporting *ipsissima verba*. This is the Jesus speaking in his own members as they engage in mystical reflections on his saving message for them. The language is very simple, almost childlike in its short plain statements, but rich in its simplicity.

So Jesus' long discourse to Nicodemus begins: "Jesus answered and said to him: 'Can you be a teacher in Israel and not understand this? In all truth I tell you:

'We say what we know,
   and bear witness to what we have seen
   and you cannot cope with our witness.
If you do not believe
   when I tell you of things on earth,
how will you believe
   when I tell you of things in heaven?
And no one has mounted up into heaven
   if not the one who has come down from heaven—
   the Son of Man.
And just as Moses lifted up the serpent in the desert,
   so must the Son of Man be lifted up,
that all who put their trust in him
   may have in him a life that never ends.
For God so loved the world
   that he gave over the Son, the only-begotten,
lest any putting trust in him should perish,
   but may have a life that never ends.
For God did not dispatch his Son into the world
   in order to condemn the world,
   but that the world should be rescued through him.
Those trusting him are not condemned,
   but those who do not trust have already been condemned
   for not trusting to the title of God's only-begotten Son.
The condemnation, then, lies in this,
   that the light has come into the world
and men loved the darkness more than the light,
   since their actions were evil.

For the one whose actions are evil
   must hate the light,
and does not come near the light
   lest his acts be exposed.
But one who enacts the truth
   comes near to the light
that his acts may be exposed,
   how they were performed in God.'" (3.11–21)

At the end of this discourse, nothing is said about the reaction of Nicodemus. When next we encounter him (7.50–52), he is still not entirely committed to Jesus, but he tells his fellow members of the Sanhedrin that they should at least hear what he has to say for himself before condemning him. They respond sarcastically: "Don't tell us you are from Galilee too." That was meant to shut him up, and for all we know it did. At least temporarily. But he puts in a last appearance with all his doubts removed. He joins Joseph of Arimathea in burying the body of Jesus (19.39–40). Significantly, both men were hearers of Jesus who had not, to this point, openly professed him. We know of Nicodemus's clandestine approach, and John now tells us that Joseph, too, was "a follower of Jesus, but a hidden one, since he feared the Jews" (19.38). Brown says: "John may be hinting that crypto-believers in the synagogue of his own time should follow the example of Joseph and Nicodemus" (2B 960).

It was an act of extraordinary courage for two such prominent men to care for the body of a crucified man, who was unclean and could not undergo proper burial with those who were unpolluted—hence the "new" or unused tomb (19.41). In defiance of custom, the two prominent men give Jesus a full Jewish burial, wrapped in a cloth and anointed with aromatic spices, the latter brought by Nicodemus in extraordinary quantity—a hundred pounds (19.39)! This seems to be another example of John's seeing Messianic-age excess of good things, a surplus of loving care like the huge surplus of wine Jesus supplied at Cana. There is a guarantee of Jesus' proper burial, even against the cleanliness taboo, in the fact that Nicodemus was a Pharisee and a member of the Sanhedrin, who would not omit proper burial procedure.

In giving Jesus this anointment, John is ignoring the account of all three Synoptics—that Jesus was hurried to burial and the women had to bring oils and spices for his anointing on the morning after the feast. One can assume that the women may not have known how Jesus was buried by Joseph and Nicodemus. But John allows for a woman's anointment in the account of Mary of Bethany laving his feet six days before Passover (12.1–8). That, too, was an act of excess. The perfumes used were worth three hundred silver pieces, and they filled the whole house with their aroma. Judas objects to the expense, but Jesus defends the Messianic excess: "Give in to her. Should she save it to anoint me at the tomb?"[1]

Woman at the Well

THIS, LIKE THOSE of Nicodemus and Lazarus, is an episode only John contains. Many think it reflects a general awareness and sensitivity to Samaritans in the tradition of the Beloved Disciple. It was a deep insult for some Jews to call Jesus himself "possessed and a Samaritan" (8.48). Significantly, Jesus denies that he is possessed but not that he is Samaritan. As we saw earlier, in the discussion of Luke, hostility between Samaritans and Jerusalem was such as to make each consider the other impure and profane for worshiping at the wrong Temple. The Temple of the Samaritans was on Mount Gerizim, and the area around it was considered unclean by the Jews. It was risking pollution for Jesus even to come near it. One time when he tried this, he was repelled by the Samaritans themselves (Lk 9.52–53). When he succeeds in getting near Gerizim in John, he encounters all by himself a woman who is many times over unclean. She is not only a Samaritan but a woman who has had five husbands and is currently living with a man who is not her husband.

She is astonished that he would talk with her, especially since they are alone, and his followers are shocked when they catch up with him and find him speaking to an unaccompanied woman—and such a woman. But in fact he had asked her to bring water up from the well in her dipper. She warns him that her handling of the vessel makes it unclean by Jerusalem standards. "How can you, who are a Jew, ask for a drink from me, a Samaritan woman?" (4.9). John adds here an explanatory note: "Jews, that is to say, have no communion with Samaritans." The point John spells out Jesus seems not to get. Instead of discussing the Holiness Code, he surprisingly answers:

"If you recognized God's bounty
   and who is asking a drink from you,
you would have asked him,
   and he would have given you a water that lives." (4.10)

It is a common technique of John's Gospel to bring out a deeper meaning in exchanges by having Jesus' interlocutor take his words on a surface level, which he then goes below—to show the hidden riches of the teaching. So the onlookers took the Temple he would rebuild as the Jerusalem structure, not his body. Nicodemus misunderstood "higher birth" as mere fleshly rebirth, not spiritual birth. The crowds will misunderstand the bread he offers. So, here, the Samaritan woman thinks he is offering her the same kind of water she could draw up for him. She says: "Sir, you have no dipper, and this well is deep. How then can you draw up this water that lives? You are clearly not greater than our father Jacob, who gave us this well, and who drank from it himself, as his sons and flocks did" (4.11–12). Then Jesus tells her it is an inner spring, a refreshment of the soul, that he refers to, one fed by his own interior riches as a conduit to the Father.

"Whoever takes a drink from this water
   will be thirsty for it again.
But one who drinks the water I shall give him
   will not thirst again forever.
No, that water I give him
   will be in him a fountain
springing up into endless life." (4.13–14)

When the woman asks how to drink of this inner fountain, Jesus tells her to summon her husband. When she admits she has none, he tells her what husbands she has had. She acknowledges him as a prophet, but asks how he can prophesy at Gerizim when he honors another Temple. Once again she has misunderstood the power of the new prophecy, which is not associated with any earthly Temple. Her misunderstanding brings forth the heart of Jesus' new message.

> "Have trust in me, woman,
>> the hour comes,
> when neither on this mountain
>> nor in Jerusalem
>> will you give honor to the Father.
> You Samaritans honor blindly,
>> while we see what we honor,
>> since rescue is from the Jews.
> But an hour approaches,
>> and is now arrived,
> when those who honor truly
>> will honor the Father in Spirit and truth.
> No wonder, since those honoring so
>> are what the Father seeks.
> God is himself Spirit,
>> and those honoring him
>> must honor him in Spirit and truth." (4.21–24)

The woman says that she expects such things when the Messiah comes, and Jesus says, "I who speak with you, I AM."

His revelation comes to the woman, the outcast, the unclean. Jesus has broken through every conceivable barrier to gather the entirety of the lost to him.

The words to the Samaritan about a "water that lives" will be taken up again when Jesus goes to Jerusalem for the Feast of Tabernacles, during whose ceremonies the waters of purification were a subject of song (2B 322–23). There he tells onlookers:

> "If anyone should thirst, let him come to me
> And let him drink as he puts his trust in me.
> For aptly the Sacred Writings say:
> 'Rivers of waters that live flow from his depths.' "
> (7.37–38)

Scholars have puzzled over the quotation from the Sacred Writings in that last line. No exact source can be found. Raymond Brown argues cogently that the reference is to the many places where it is said that Moses struck a rock and water gushed out to ease the thirst of the Jews wandering through the desert (2B 322–23).

That Jesus was the rock from which saving water flows was an early Christian belief that Paul could appeal to (1 Corinthians 10.4). This was the most frequent symbol used in the art of the catacombs. Its meaning would have been instantly obvious to the Johannine community.[2]

The Adulteress

ALL FOUR OF the episodes considered in this chapter—those dealing with Nicodemus, with the Samaritan Woman, with the adulteress, and with Lazarus—occur only in John's Gospel, and in a sense the adulteress does not occur even there.

She is missing from the earliest manuscripts of John. She was first accepted into the Gospel in the West (by, among others, Ambrose and Jerome and Augustine), though the story seems to have come from the East. Raymond Brown follows the suggestion that the story was too "liberal" to be accepted at once: "The ease with which Jesus forgave the adulteress was hard to reconcile with the stern penitential discipline in vogue in the early church" (2B 335). Since it was included in Jerome's Vulgate Latin Bible, it was accepted as canonical in the Middle Ages. The Byzantine church and the King James Version also accept it, giving it an ecumenical sweep of Catholic, Orthodox, and Protestant traditions. There was at least one redactor who expanded John's Gospel, so it would not be surprising if a further addition were made, and from the same trove of teachings by the Beloved Disciple.

Some object to this last point, since the story seems in style and theme more like Luke than John, and some manuscripts actually put it in Luke's Gospel rather than John's. But its place in John reflects other passages on judgment in this chapter (8), where Jesus says, "You are judges by fleshly standards, but I am no one's judge" (8.15), and, "Can any of you convict me of sin?" (8.46). Besides, the Johannine theme of escape

179

from external and ceremonial norms to the inner state is borne out in the story as in the other episodes dealt with here.

A question of fact obtrudes. Was this woman subject to the Law of Moses calling for her death by stoning? John's Gospel denies that the Jews under Roman rule had the power of execution *(jus gladii)*. That is why the Jews must turn Jesus over to Pilate for the Roman form of the death penalty (crucifixion) rather than the Jews' execution technique (lapidation)—when Pilate tells the Jews to execute Jesus, they answer: "Putting any to death is not permitted us" (18.31). This is one of the accurate facts that John knows and the other evangelists do not (2B 848–50). This need not affect the story of the adulteress. The Jews are not actually represented as on the point of stoning her. They ask Jesus whether the Law of Moses should apply to her—which would involve stoning her *if* that were still possible. The aim of this story, as of many others, is to show certain Jews trying to trap Jesus. If he denies the Law of Moses, even hypothetically, he is committing a religious offense. If he advises execution, against the Roman ban, he is committing a political offense. Either way, he seems to have no out. John spells this out explicitly: "They spoke as a way of putting him to the test, so they could have a charge to bring against him" (8.6).

Jesus' response is brilliant. At first he says nothing, but engages in a prophetic action—he bends over and draws something in the dirt with his finger. When the questioners persist, he delivers an answer that neither affirms the Mosaic Law nor defies the Roman restriction. Again, he goes to an inner truth. Even if the Law were in effect, could a person not free of sin execute it? "Let any one of you who is sinless be the first to stone her" (8.7). He is not necessarily describing an imminent stoning. He is responding to the hypothetical they had proposed him. *If* the Law of Moses were still in effect, could any one of them execute it? Jesus then bent over again and wrote on the ground. While he was doing this, all the accusers slipped away, leaving Jesus alone with the adulteress. When he straightens up, he asks, "Woman, where are they? Is no one here to condemn you?" She answers, "None, sir," and he continues: "Neither do I condemn you. Leave, and sin no more" (8.10–11).

What was Jesus writing? Many fanciful answers have been given to this question. Some claim he was writing the sins of the accusers, who read them and fled. This involves an unlikely quantity of writing and jostling to read. Besides, it would not explain the first time he writes in the dust, which happened before he mentioned the accusers' sins. Others think he is writing some text from the Sacred Writings (there are several candidates for the one chosen). But who is to recognize the words, and draw their meaning? We are not told that he formed words, and if they were important to the story John would presumably indicate what they were. In an oral culture, writing was a less effective response than spoken words, as Socrates maintained. When a prophet makes some symbolic gesture, the *action* is what matters. Jesus feigns indifference to the question posed in bad faith. When it is insisted on again, he gives his cryptic answer and bends down again to show that he will not dignify their attempts at entrapment. The fact that he blanks them out of his attention is seen from his first words when he straightens up and asks, "Where are they?" He has ignored them away, as their disingenuous plot deserves. But he does not answer *her* in a riddle. He tells her that their sinfulness should not be taken as a license for her to sin more. He ignores the ritual impurity she has incurred, which should prevent him from even speaking with her. He has come to preach the true inner purity of communion with the Father. This is a story worthy of the Gospel it ended up in, however it ended up there.

Lazarus

THE RAISING OF Lazarus occurs just before the Passion narrative, and explains its climax. Giving Lazarus life was something Jesus had to pay for with his own life. It is what infuriates the Temple authorities, who see it is a claim to be the Messiah (11.47–48). This episode has the same function in John that the agony in the garden of Gethsemane does in the Synoptics. It shows Jesus facing his own death, and rebelling against it. In the garden on the eve of his death, says Mark (14.33), Jesus began to feel terrified *(ekthambeisthai)* and helpless *(adēmonein)*. He tells the three followers he has taken with him deeper into the garden, "I am in misery *(perilypos)* to the point of death." According to Luke (22.44), "And struggling as he was, he kept praying more earnestly, and his sweat fell in separate drops to the ground as if it were blood." The only other time Jesus suffered such physical symptoms before his actual Passion was when he confronted the death of Lazarus (Jn 11.33). As he approached those mourning the death of his friend, "he was convulsed *(enebrimēsato)* and loosed his passion *(etaraxen heauton)."* After he broke into tears, he went to the tomb itself and was "once more convulsed *(palin embrimōmenos)"* (11.38).

What explains this agony? He faces his own death as he wrenches Lazarus free from death. When Lazarus's sisters called for him while their brother was dying, he knew he was returning to the killing zone. His followers tell him, "Teacher, just now the Jews were trying to stone you there, and are you returning?" (11.8). When he says he must go, Thomas speaks up with characteristic bravado, "Go we along too, we shall die with him" (11.16). But Jesus is still following the Father's schedule for "my time," so he delays—just as he put off his mother's call to work a miracle at Cana. His hour has not come, though it is coming:

> Jesus told them: "Daylight lasts only twelve hours, does it not? If a man walks by daylight, he does not stumble, since he sees by the light of this world. But if a man walks in the night, he stumbles, since there is no light in him." (11.9–10)

The approach of his own sunset sets the mood for his restoration of Lazarus from the dark. His words reflect Jeremiah 13.16:

> Ascribe glory to the Lord your God
>   before the darkness falls,
>   before your feet stumble
>   on the twilit hillsides.

When Jesus finally sets off for Bethany, Lazarus has been dead for four days. His sister Mary, learning of the approach of Jesus, goes out to meet him. She says that if he had come earlier, Lazarus would not have died. Jesus answers her, as so often, with a deeper meaning for "life." He means eternal life. (But just as at Cana, he will give a lower sign of the higher reality when he raises Lazarus.)

Jesus tells her, "Your brother will rise again."

Martha tells him, "I realize that he will rise again at the resurrection on the last day."

Jesus declared to her, "I am the resurrection and the life. Whoever trusts in me, though he die, will live, and everyone who lives with trust in me will not ever die. Do you have this trust?"

She says to him, "Yes, Lord, I have reached the trust that you are the Messiah, the Son of God, the one coming into the world." (11.23–27)

Martha then summons her sister, Mary (the less activist sibling had not run out to Jesus), and they go Lazarus's tomb, which is a cave sealed with a stone. When Jesus says, "Take the stone away," Martha protests that, after four days, the body must stink.

Martin Scorsese, in his film *The Last Temptation of Christ*, dramatizes what the Gospel has been saying about Jesus' reluctance to re-enter the killing zone around Jerusalem, his convulsive reaction to another's death, his posing of the issue of eternal life and death. Jesus is taking on the power of death, in a personal struggle like that dramatized by Matthew and Luke as the trial in the desert. Scorsese shows Jesus reaching into the tomb to pull Lazarus out; but the dead hand almost pulls Jesus in with it. Jesus is symbolically entering his own grave, giving life to another by laying down his own. This struggle at the boundaries of life is won only by great effort.

People naturally ask what happened to Lazarus when he came back to life.

We are not told anything more about Lazarus, other than that he ate with Jesus six days before the Passover, and that the chief priests resolved to end the rejoicing over Lazarus's restoration by killing him (12.2, 10). Since the mourners at Lazarus's tomb remark on how Jesus loved the man (11.36), some have tried to identify Lazarus with the Beloved Disciple. But Brown rightly asks why Lazarus is named and the much loved follower is not (2B xcv). The meaning of Lazarus for us is the way he dramatizes the life of the baptized Christian. We have all died into Jesus and risen again, even in this life, as Paul put it at Romans 6.2–4:

> How can we who died to sin continue to live in sin? Or do you not realize that we, those baptized into Messiah Jesus, were baptized into his death? We were laid in the grave with him by our baptism into death, so that, just as Messiah was raised from the dead in the splendor of the Father, we may journey on in renewed life.

Followers of Jesus are the dead and the living. He daily wrestles us free from the grip of death. We have gone into the tomb and come back. We are Lazarus.

NOTES

1. Later manuscripts of John add here a verse from Matthew, a Gospel John did not know: "The poor you have with you always, but you will not have me with you always."

2. By recognizing that the reference is to the rock of Moses, we solve another dispute: is the person from whose depths (literally "gut," *koilia*) the water flows the believer, or Jesus? The understanding of Jesus as the rock symbolized in Exodus makes it clear that he is the source of the waters—as he will be on the cross, when water flows from his side (Jn 19.34) as it flowed from the side of the rock.

12. Life Out of Death

ALL FOUR GOSPELS say that Jesus, on his last trip to Jerusalem, entered the city riding a donkey, to the acclaim of a crowd. The Synoptics treat this as a royal reception, though it is not clear why the crowd expected Jesus to be the king of Israel. In all three, Jesus knows ahead of time where the donkey will be found, and sends two disciples to secure it and bring it to him. Then the disciples spread their own garments on the donkey as a kind of honorific saddle. Once Jesus is mounted, the disciples and others spread garments on the ground as what would now be called a processional red carpet. In Luke (19.35), only the garments are laid down. In Mark (11.8), boughs are added to the clothing. In Matthew (21.8), leaves are scattered.

John tells a very different story. Jesus does not send disciples ahead to bring him the donkey. The crowds are already worked to a high pitch by the raising of Lazarus. Some come along from Bethany, where the sensation arose. Others, hearing of the miracle, come out from the city waving palms, a victory symbol. A third crowd joins in, made up of Pharisees and high priests critical of the other two crowds. Jesus, responding to this fevered scene, finds a donkey on the spot and on his own, and mounts it as a gesture of humility. This is the Gospel in which Jesus will tell Pilate that his reign is not of the present order. His mounting of the donkey is a prophetic gesture protesting the triumphalist attitude of those bearing palms. "The large crowd has misunderstood the Lazarus miracle" (2B 462).The palms occur only in John's Gospel, where Jesus rejects what they symbolize. Later Palm Sunday celebrations have got it all wrong.

The Last Supper

IN A FURTHER gesture of humility, Jesus plays the servant when he begins his last meal with the followers, washing their feet. This is one of the many details of the Last Supper that John alone reports, on the word of the Beloved Disciple, who is mentioned here for the first time (13.23). The interplay of the characters at the Last Supper as John describes it is very dramatic. In order to follow this series of exchanges we must dismiss the image of the Last Supper imprinted on our culture by Leonardo and his imitators, the picture of diners upright on one side of a straight table. At a normal dinner of the time, people reclined on three couches—one couch behind a central table and two couches behind flanking tables at right angles to the central one. The diners were served by people moving in the space between the flanking tables. Raymond Brown argues from the dramaturgy of the scene John describes that the Beloved Disciple was on Jesus' right side on the central couch, Judas was on his left, and Peter was at the far end of the flanking table on Jesus' right. Jesus washes Peter's feet last, which indicates that he worked around the couches from the one on his left to the one in the center to the one on his right.

The washing of the feet is normally and understandably taken as a lesson to the followers that they should be servants of one another. But Raymond Brown sees that Jesus is doing what he does because "having loved his chosen ones in this present order, he loved them all the way to the goal *(eis telos)."* What the goal is he makes clear on the cross when, at the moment of his death, he says, "The goal is reached" *(tetelestai).* Jesus is saying not only that the followers should wash one another's feet but that they should be willing to die for one another—a continuation of the theme in the Lazarus story, that death is the path to life. Life and death are locked in a struggle through the whole last part of this Gospel, and life wins only by losing to death. That is the paradox of the Gospel. It is also the theme of the long Last Discourse at the final supper.

That Brown's is the proper reading of the feet-washing scene is confirmed by what Jesus will say in the course of the Last Supper. He says, for instance:

"A fresh directive I give you,
   love one another.
As I have loved you,
   you must love one another." (13.34)

Augustine asks how it can be a fresh directive (or "new commandment") to love one another, when the Law had said, "You shall love your neighbor as a man like yourself" (Leviticus 19.18)?[1] He said that several things make the directive new when Jesus issues it on the night of his arrest. How was he loving them? He is about to say:

> "Greater love than this has no one,
>> that he give his life for his dear ones." (15.13)

If, therefore, they are to love one another as he loves them, they must be willing to die for one another.

What Jesus directs them to do is new, as well, because the love he enjoins is not simply a natural affection but a manifestation of the Father's love as coursing through them. "As my Father has loved me, so I have loved you" (15.9). It is the Father's own love circulating through Jesus to the disciples and back through him to the Father. "I am the vine, and you the branches" (15.5). That is why their flourishing "manifests the Father's splendor" (15.8). Engrafted onto the vine of Jesus, the disciples are in effect a new creation. So Augustine says that they live with a fresh directive because they are "new men, heirs of a new covenant, singers of a new song."[2] Their dying into Jesus will reanimate each other.

The Beloved Disciple at the Last Supper

THE RECLINING POSTURE made it easy for the Beloved Disciple to lay his head on Jesus' chest (a clumsy move for those sitting upright). When Jesus announces that one of them will betray him, Peter, at the end of the flanking table, "nodded to him [the Beloved Disciple] and said, 'Ask who it is he means'" (13.24). This is where the Beloved Disciple leans on Jesus' chest, so no one will hear their exchange. Judas, on the other side, clearly does not hear it. Jesus tells the Beloved Disciple, "It is the one I give this bit of food to after I dip it in the dish" (13.26). Judas takes the morsel without knowing that it identifies him as the betrayer. The Beloved Disciple is close enough to hear what Jesus tells Judas in a lowered voice after he accepts the bit of food: "What you do, do quickly" (13.27).

The Beloved Disciple is named here, because only he can know of his own whispered exchange with Jesus and the soft words to Judas. Why does John not mention the Beloved Disciple until the last events in his Gospel? Had the man only recently joined the followers? John says that the Beloved Disciple will live longer than the other followers (21.23–24). The Beloved Disciple was probably young, then, perhaps extremely young, a teenager. The very name "the follower whom Jesus loved" does not mean that Jesus loved only him. It suggests a nickname, as if the young recruit were a kind of mascot, who romps around, the pet of the company. Some have suggested that he was the young man in Mark who ran away naked from the scene of Jesus' arrest (Mk 14.51–52). If so, it was typical that he would run from the scene when Peter cut off the attendant's ear. In John, he is always mentioned in conjunction with Peter, with only one exception, when he stands at the cross with the mother of Jesus, in Peter's absence (19.25–27).

Before that, he is the one Peter gets to ask Jesus who will betray him (13.24). He and Peter are the only male followers who run to the empty tomb, and he outruns the older man (20.3–4). He is the one whose eyesight is best at the Sea of Tiberias, when he recognizes Jesus on the shore and tells Peter who it is (21.7). He is the one Peter asks about when Jesus predicts the death of Peter (21.18–22). He is the one who is offered as the best witness for all these actions (21.24). If he was not yet part of the company when Jesus chose the first disciples, or when he singled out the Twelve, that would explain why the other evangelists do not mention him.

The Last Discourse

THE COMMUNITY that was formed by the Beloved Disciple reflected on the details he knew so intimately, and on the deeper meaning of Jesus' words. At the Last Supper, John's account builds, in wave after wave of redaction, the long Last Discourse. Augustine and others have found the purest distillation of Jesus' meaning in these words.

"This is my directive,
　　that you love one another
　　as I have loved you.
Greater love than this has no one,
　　that he give his life for his dear ones.
You are my dear ones
　　since you heed my directives.

I no longer call you my slaves,
   for a slave does not understand the master's acts,
but I call you my dear ones,
      since all I know from the Father
      I have shared with you.
You have not singled me out,
      I have singled you out,
and I support you in your course,
      a course that will abound,
      and your abundance will abide,
so that, ask what you will from the Father,
      he will give it to you to honor my title." (15.12–16)

The intimate tie Jesus has with the Father he also has with his followers. They meet the Father in him, and he in them.

"I am the vine
      and you the branches.
One engrafted in me, and I in him,
      bears a great harvest. . . .
If you are engrafted in me,
      and my words are engrafted in you,
ask whatever you will,
      and it will be done for you.
This manifests my Father's splendor,
      that your harvest abound,
      and you be my followers.
As my Father loves me
      so I love you." (15.5, 7–9)

This long speech at the end of Jesus' life (over three chapters of the Gospel) is like the long Sermon on the Mount at the beginning of his public ministry in Matthew (three chapters also). Each sums up the major teachings of its Gospel. That John's discourse is built up by the redactor with additions and repetitions is manifested in its several "false endings," most notably at 14.31, "Rise and let us go." Yet the entire Discourse has a more intimate feel than the Sermon on the Mount, since the death of Jesus is felt impending throughout. The urgency that is conveyed is the finest bequest of the Beloved Disciple to his own school. As Raymond Brown says, this is Jesus still speaking to his followers through and beyond his death.

> Although he speaks at the Last Supper, he is really speaking from heaven; although those who hear him are his disciples, his words are directed to Christians of all times. The Last Discourse is Jesus' last testament: It is meant to be read after he has left the earth. Yet it is not like other last testaments, which are the recorded words of men who are dead and can speak no more; for whatever there may be of *ipsissima verba* in the Last Discourse has been transformed in the light of the Resurrection and through the coming of the Paraclete into a living discourse delivered not by a dead man, but by the one who has life, to all readers of the Gospel. (2B 582)

One of the most important pledges of the Last Supper, in terms of the continuing instruction Brown talks of, is the promise of the Paraclete:

"If you love me,

you will heed my directives,

and I will ask the Father

and he will send you another Champion,

who will stay with you through all time,

the Spirit of Truth." (14.15–17)

The word "Paraclete" literally means "called to one's side" (para-klētos). It refers to one who will champion your cause. Why does Jesus says that this is *another* Champion? The answer is that Jesus is himself the disciples' Champion, as we learn from another writing of the Beloved Disciple's school: "Should anyone sin, we have a champion (paraklētos) before the Father, Jesus Messiah, upholding the right" (1 John 2.1). Or as Augustine put it, "Jesus is himself a defender, since the Latin for paraclete is defender (advocatus)."³ Jesus is his followers' Champion. He says now that he is returning to the Father, but they are not abandoned. He and the Father are sending a Champion who will stay with them. That is how he comforts them before being taken away from them.

The Passion

THE AGONY IN the garden is not in John's Gospel, though Jesus accepts the cup of suffering that he prays to avoid in the Synoptics (18.11). John places all his emphasis on the divinity of Jesus as he goes through the Passion. He is not passive but active in accepting his ordeal. Judas leads the Roman cohort and the Temple police to the secret place he knew, where the high priests had bribed him to arrange for the arrest of Jesus out of the public gaze. But Jesus does not submit to a kiss from Judas in this account. Jesus, who had told Judas to do what he had to do quickly, knows what is coming, and he takes the initiative: "Thus Jesus, in full knowledge of what was coming, went forward, and says: 'Who is it you come after?'" (18.4). When they say Jesus of Nazareth is their prey, he tells them, "I AM," and as Judas stands by, "they recoiled and fell down" (18.5–6). As the soldiers are regrouping themselves, Peter strikes off the attendant's ear, and Jesus says: "Put the sword back in its holder. Am I not to drink the cup my Father proffers me?" (18.11).

The arresting soldiers are presumably put at the disposal of the high priests by Pilate so they can keep order in the Passover crowds. They take Jesus, not to the high priest himself but to his father-in-law, Annas, the former high priest. There will be no formal trial of Jesus before the Sanhedrin in this Gospel. The details of Peter's action at the court of Annas are more detailed in John, presumably because the Beloved Disciple learned them from Peter. He knows, for instance, that Peter was able to enter Annas's courtyard because "another disciple" knew Annas and vouched for him. Why would a follower of Jesus either know Annas or have any influence on his guards at the courtyard? Remember that Nicodemus is an important figure in John's Gospel, first as a covert inquirer after Jesus' teaching and finally as an open follower who helps bury him. In 7.51, when the priests were plotting against Jesus, he had said that the man should at least be given a hearing. They had responded, "Are you too from Galilee?" (7.52).

It is the same taunt that Peter is about to hear: "Are you too one of his followers?" (18.17).

It seems, then, that Nicodemus, not yet a confessed disciple, smuggled Peter past the guards into the courtyard as he went himself to observe the proceedings of his peers in the priestly circle. What occurred in the chamber of Annas could have been related to the Beloved Disciple by Nicodemus, who seems to have become one of the "Johannine" community, which alone preserves his memory. Another detail known only to the Beloved Disciple's tradition is that Peter was identified in the courtyard by a relative of Malchus, the man whose ear Peter cut off (18.26). Only John's Gospel names Malchus.

There is no formal proceeding by the Sanhedrin in John's Gospel, just a hugger-mugger questioning before Annas— which makes John, at least in this respect, less anti-Semitic than the Synoptics. When, later, Jesus tells Pilate that the Roman is less guilty in executing him than the man who "turned me over" (19.11), that is taken by some to refer to Annas or Caiaphas. But the betrayer (ho paradidous) is regularly Judas in the Gospels—a Jew, certainly, but a follower of Jesus. As we shall see, the betrayers of Peter and Paul would also be fellow followers of Jesus. Jesus is killed by his own, then as now.

Annas lets his son-in-law, Caiaphas, take Jesus to Pilate and demand his death. As Brown points out, Jesus puts Pilate on trial, rather than vice versa. He uses the same counterquestioning technique that he used with the Pharisees who tried to entrap him. John is dramatizing the real power relations

that exist between Jesus and the man who thinks he has control of him. Jesus is allowing the use of human power while
abdicating his divine power. When Pilate asks if Jesus is a king,
he answers: "My reign is not of this present order. If my reign
were of this present order, my supporters would be struggling
for me, to prevent the Jews from turning me over. But my
reign is not here" (18.36). Pilate misunderstands, as the
worldly-minded always do in John's Gospel. "Does that mean
you are a king?" Jesus answers: "You say I am a king. What
I was born for, and why I entered this present order, was to
give testimony to the truth. All on the side of truth hear my
voice" (18.37). And Pilate condemns himself with his remark:
"What is truth?"

Pilate tries to fob Barabbas off on the crowd. He even tries
to appeal to its mercy by displaying the flogged and brutal-
ized Jesus to them, hoping they will take this as a final punishment. "Just look at the man" (19.5). But the mob threatens
Pilate with blackmail, saying it will turn him in to his imperial superiors for allowing a political threat to go unpunished:
"If you release this man, you are not loyal to Caesar. Anyone
claiming kingship of his own opposes Caesar" (19.12). Pilate
yields to this reason of state. He is the prisoner of his own
power.

Jesus is still in control as he goes to his death. In John, he
carries his own cross. After being lifted up on the cross, he
sees four women and one man—the Beloved Disciple—standing by, and his mother is among them. To her he says, "Look,
woman—your son." And to the Beloved Disciple, "Look—
your mother." John adds: "And from that time he took her

into his charge" (19.26–27). It might seem strange that Jesus would entrust his mother's care to a young and recent addition to his following. But the glimpse we get of the young John suggests that he was athletic and resourceful. He may have had a home in Jerusalem, unlike the followers who had come with Jesus from Galilee. He may also have been a favorite of Mary, as he was of Jesus and Peter.

There were only two other sayings from the cross, according to John. The first, "I thirst," was said to be in accord with the Sacred Writings, because "he was aware that the goal was reached, to bring the Sacred Writings to their completion"—since the soldiers offer him wine on a hyssop wand, which was used to sprinkle the blood of the Paschal lamb on the doorposts of the Israelites, effecting their deliverance (Exodus 12.22). When Jesus sips the wine on the hyssop he has completed the drinking of that cup the Father gave him (18.11), and he gives up his life with the words "The goal is reached" (19.30). The goal *(telos)* was clear to Jesus from the outset. He moved toward it indeflectibly. His mission was to die, but on the Father's schedule. He moved according to his time *(kairos)*. God himself was joining the democracy of man's death.

In keeping with the Paschal imagery of this death, the bones of Jesus, like that of the Paschal lamb, are not broken. Instead, a soldier pierces his side, "and straightway blood and water flowed out" (19.34). We have already seen that the favorite image for Jesus in early Christian art was the rock that gushed water when Moses touched it with his rod. Speaking to the woman at the well, Jesus had applied the prophet's words to himself: "Rivers of waters that live flow from his depths" (7.38). Here blood joins the water, enforcing the image of waters that live. The water and blood symbolize the revivifying life from death that Jesus brings to humankind. Augustine notes that Jesus is the vine and the vine sends out sustenance through the branches.[4] The water and blood from his side are a kind of sap shed from the vine. Augustine also thought there might be a parallel between the opening of the first Adam's side to create Eve, and the opening of the second Adam's side to create his "bride," the body of his believers.[5] The Beloved Disciple, who was standing at the cross, tells us that he saw the actual piercing of Jesus' side: "The one who saw it has now testified, and his testimony is true, and he is aware that he speaks true in order that even you can trust it. For this all happened to fulfill the Sacred Writings."

The Resurrection

THOUGH JOHN NAMES the four women who stood by the cross (19.25), he describes only one of them, Mary Magdalene, as going to the tomb early on Sunday morning. When she finds it empty, she thinks that someone has stolen the body (so little did she expect a resurrection), and she runs to tell Peter.

> So Peter set off, along with the other disciple, and they went to the tomb. But they were running along together and the other disciple ran faster than Peter and reached the tomb first.

And leaning down he looks at the winding cloths lying there, but he did not enter. Then Simon Peter arrives, following him, and he entered the tomb. And he inspects the winding cloths lying there, and the veil for covering the face, not with the winding cloths but apart, folded up in its own location. Only then did the other disciple, who had arrived first at the tomb, enter it. And he saw and took on trust, for they did not yet understand the Sacred Writings, that he must rise from the dead. (20.3–9)

The Beloved Disciple again shows his swiftness of comprehension. He is the first to believe, though Peter and others still suspect that the body was stolen. The Beloved Disciple describes the condition of the cerements so exactly, since a grave robber would not be likely to remove the cloths and place them so neatly. The Beloved Disciple comes into the tomb later than Peter but understands its meaning before him. He is faster not only at running but at comprehending.

Mary Magdalene is back near the tomb, distraught and weeping, when she sees a person she takes to be the gardener—a difficulty at recognizing the risen Jesus that is experienced by almost all the disciples. When the dim figure asks why she weeps, she says:

"Sir, if you are the one who took him away, tell me where you have put him so I may take him up." Jesus says to her, "Mary." Turning closer, she calls him in Aramaic, "Rabboni" (which means Teacher). Jesus says to her, "Do not hold on to me, since I have not yet gone up to my Father. But go to my brothers and tell them, 'I am going up to my Father and your Father, and my God and your God.' " (20.15–17)

Mary Magdalene was clearly an important figure for the community of the Beloved Disciple. Here she becomes the second person to believe in the risen Jesus, second only to the Beloved Disciple himself. And she becomes the first to report to the other disciples that she has seen the Lord. This probably reflects an actual preaching role Mary had played in the history of the Johannine community.

Jesus appears to the disciples, who are in hiding behind locked doors, and assures them that the Spirit is now with them, fulfilling his promise to have his Father send the Paraclete. But the disciple Thomas was not present when Jesus first appeared to them. He refused to believe them when they told him about the appearance. "I believe not until I see the trace of the nails in his hands and thrust my finger into the trace of the nails and thrust my hand into his side" (20.25). When Jesus appears again while Thomas is with the others, he tells him to probe his wounds, but Thomas responds, "My Lord and my God." Great works of art—especially Verrocchio's statue and Caravaggio's painting—show Thomas putting his finger into Christ's side. But he never does that in the Gospel. He responds to Jesus' words with an instant profession of his trust, and Jesus says, "You have trust in me because you have seen me. Happy those who see me not and still have trust" (20.29).

The Gospel originally ended at 20.30–31: "Many indeed

were the other miraculous things Jesus did in the company of his followers, which are not set down in this book. But these have been set down that you may have trust that Jesus is the Messiah, the Son of God, and that holding this trust you may have life by the power of his title." But the redactor of the Gospel adds a whole new section, as usual not trying to disguise his intervention by changing the original or canceling its first ending. Since the new section speaks of the death of the Beloved Disciple, it may be that the Gospel originally ended while that long-lived man was still alive.

The epilogue tells of appearances to the disciples after they have returned to Galilee. They are out fishing when a man calls from the shore to ask after their catch. When they say there has been none, he tells them to cast their net to the right of the boat. The net comes up full, and the Beloved Disciple tells Peter that it is the Lord who called out to them. Peter, impetuous as always, leaps into the water to get to Jesus. The Beloved Disciple, for once, is not so fast. He works with the others to bring in the catch. Once they are on shore, Jesus eats with them.

Then Jesus asks Peter three times if he loves him, and when Peter professes his love as often as he had denied Jesus, he is told to feed the Lord's sheep. And Jesus adds:

"In all truth I tell you, as a young fellow you hitched up your garment and strolled wherever you would, but in your age you will extend your hands, and another will hitch you up and bear you off against your will." He said this to indicate the kind of death by which he would pay tribute to the splendor of God. And having told him that, he says, "Follow me." (21.18–19)

The legend of Peter said that he would die by crucifixion, and would ask to die upside down, as unworthy to imitate his Savior. (Actually, upside-down crucifixion, by forcing the blood to the head, would lead to a swifter and so easier death.) The earliest direct reference to Peter's death is in a letter from Clement of Rome to the gathering in Corinth. He says that Peter died from "rivalry and grudge" among the Brothers, but does not say how he was executed. Tacitus reports that the Christians killed by Nero were turned in by their fellows, and they were killed in ingeniously original ways. Crucifixion was normal, not original. Nero invented two new methods for killing the Christians—"dogs tore them apart after they were sewn up in animal skins . . . or, after nightfall, they were set on fire to serve as lamps" (*Annals* 15.44). Either form of death would fit the vague terms used in the Gospel of John, and obviously the early Christians did not want to get more specific about the shameful death caused by betrayal from one's own—even though that is how Jesus himself died.

Peter and the Beloved Disciple are normally considered together, so the fate of the latter is brought up too.

Turning back, Peter looks at the disciple whom Jesus loved, who was accompanying them, the one who leaned on his chest and asked, "Lord, who is your betrayer?" With him in sight, Peter says to Jesus, "Lord, what about this one?" Jesus says to him, "Should I wish for him to await my coming, what is that to you? You come with me." Thus the word spread among the Brothers and they supposed that this disciple would not die. But Jesus did not say that he would not die. He said, "Should I wish for him to await my coming, what is that to you?" This very disciple is the one testifying to these things, and his testimony we know to be true. But there were many other things that Jesus did, and if each were recorded, I doubt that the whole creation could contain all the books about them. (21.20–25)

The redactor says that the rich treasury of teachings by the Beloved Disciple is so vast that he has added only a few items from it.

NOTES

1. Augustine, *Interpreting John's Gospel* 65.1.
2. Ibid., 65.2.
3. Ibid., 74.4.
4. Ibid., 81.1.
5. Ibid., 120.2. Augustine was often the source of medieval and Renaissance iconography, and his suggestion that the church was taken from Christ's side, as Eve was from Adam's, may explain the mysterious image of Mary in Michelangelo's Sistine *Last Judgment*. The convention was that she appeared in Last Judgments as part of the *deēsis* ("pleading"), interceding with Jesus on his right side as John the Baptist does on his left side. John the Baptist is not paired with Mary in Michelangelo's fresco. She does not look to Jesus but looks down in a strange curled posture, closing in upon herself, legs and arms coiled around her. This almost fetal position she takes up directly by the wound in Jesus' side. Since Mary was often the symbol of the church, this could be a realization of Augustine's vision, the second Eve emerging from the side of the second Adam Jesus, who was her son, is now her father—whence the sonship now given over to the Beloved Disciple.

Epilogue: How to Read the Gospels

SOME PEOPLE HAVE a favorite Gospel, preferring it to the other three. For centuries Matthew was seen as the first and normative Gospel. But now Mark is seen as the first Gospel, the closest to sources. Luke has always appealed to some, for its humane stories. And John was the favorite of men like Augustine, for its theological flights and its emphasis on love.

But the churches have retained all four Gospels, and they have cycled readings from them all through the changes of yearly liturgies. Attempts to make one of them the main authority have failed ever since the second century, when Marcion declared that only Luke was genuine (mainly for its supposed connection with Paul's letters). Later in the same century, Tatian tried to discard what he considered inauthentic in his combination of the "sound" parts of the four into one narrative. He called the result of his effort the *Diatesseron*, a Greek musical term for harmony "through fours." Tatian proved no more acceptable to the orthodox tradition than Marcion. The four Gospels live.

Why are there four Gospels? Because the Christians living in different situations felt it important to draw on different aspects of Jesus' life and message. They meditated on the things that were most urgent for them as members of Jesus' mystical body. They give us four different takes on the central mystery. Mark dwells on the meaning of Jesus to his persecuted members. Matthew collects the sayings in an orderly way. Luke stresses the healing aspects of Jesus' mission. John keeps the divinity of Jesus always in mind. The highlighted qualities of the individual Gospels are present in all of them, just less emphasized in some. Since the mystery at the center of it all will never be exhausted, we need all of these angles of vision to get closer to an adequate appreciation of what Jesus means. That is why drawing from all four of them was my approach in *What Jesus Meant*.

Some think that a study of the way the Gospels were built up, their symbolism, their dependence on the Jewish Sacred Writings, will make people less devout. They even question whether a preacher should let his or her congregation in on the genetics of the Gospels. The best refutation of this view is a man who is the guiding spirit of this book. It will have escaped no one's notice how heavily I depend on the late scholar Raymond Brown (all those 1B, 2B, 3B, 4B references). I draw on him so often not only for his own great contributions to study of the New Testament, but because he so thoroughly reports, sifts, and builds on the massive scholarship of others. He offers a compendium of every opinion on every contested point in New Testament studies. Yet he remained a Sulpician priest in good standing, a man of exemplary piety as well as stunning knowledge. All his major scholarly works published in his lifetime were approved by his church's authorities (the "Nihil obstat" and the "Imprimatur"). He was hardly a radical or dissident.

I have given him the last say on so many matters that I will conclude with him here, as he speaks of the differing Passion narratives:

> When these different Passion narratives are read side by side, one should not be upset by the contrasts or ask which view of Jesus is more correct: the Marcan Jesus, who plumbs the depths of abandonment only to be vindicated; the Lucan Jesus, who worries about others and gently dispenses forgiveness; or the Johannine Jesus, who reigns victoriously from the cross in control of all that happens. All three are given to us by the inspiring Spirit, and no one of them exhausts the meaning of Jesus. It's as if one walks around a large diamond to look at it from three different angles. A true picture of the whole emerges only because the views of it are different. . . . To choose one portrayal of the crucified Jesus, in a manner that would exclude the other portrayals, or to harmonize all the Gospel portrayals into one, would deprive the cross of much of its meaning. It is important that some be able to see the head bowed in dejection, while others observe the arms outstretched in forgiveness, and still others perceive in the title on the cross the proclamation of a reigning king.[1]

How to read the Gospels? As a whole, with the reverence they derive from and address, yet with the intelligence God gave us to help us find him.

NOTES

1. Raymond E. Brown, S.S., *A Crucified Christ in Holy Week: Essays on the Four Gospel Passion Narratives* (Liturgical Press, 1986), pp. 70–71.

Acknowledgments

MY EDITOR FOR this *What X, Y, Z Meant* series is Carolyn Carlson, who started it all. My agent, Andrew Wylie, guides everything. My wife, Natalie, inspires everything.